The Creation Spirit

The Creation Spirit

AN ANTHOLOGY

Compiled by

ROBERT VAN DE WEYER
AND PAT SAUNDERS

DARTON · LONGMAN AND TODD
LONDON

First published in 1990 by
Darton, Longman and Todd Ltd
89 Lillie Road, London SW6 1UD

in association with
Little Gidding Books
Little Gidding, Huntingdon PE17 5JR

British Library Cataloguing in Publication Data

The Creation Spirit : an anthology.
  1. English literature. Special subjects. Creation.
Anthologies
  I. Van de Weyer, Robert *1950–* II. Saunders, Pat
820.80382

ISBN 0–232–51906–4

Designed by Humphrey Stone
Phototypeset by Input Typesetting Ltd,
London SW19 8DR
Printed and bound in Great Britain by
Courier International Ltd, Tiptree, Essex

Contents

Introduction

The opening of the Book of Genesis contains a vision of paradise that has captivated the western imagination for two thousand years. The vision is of a garden, laid out by God, where all manner of plants and animals, birds and fish, dwell together in harmony. And in its midst are a man and a woman whom God has appointed as stewards, to care for the garden. The creation of this beautiful garden is placed, within the Book of Genesis, at the beginning of history. Yet throughout the Bible the great prophets taught that the restoration of the garden is also the final purpose of history: that God wants to bring all his creatures again into perfect unity.

The Christian Church has sadly often betrayed this vision. As the gospel spread out into the Greek and Roman world, many new Christians tried to fuse the teachings of Christ with the fashionable 'gnostic' philosophy, which made a rigid division between the spiritual and the material realms. The object of our human life, according to this view, was for the soul to break free of all bodily, material attachments, which were seen as corrupt and evil – an attitude which, in diluted form, still permeates much Christian spirituality. Other Christians, while rejecting gnosticism, none the less tended to look down on the natural order, regarding the sole purpose of plants and animals as satisfying mankind's bodily needs. Thus the Church has in recent centuries happily con-doned the rampant exploitation of the earth's resources.

Yet throughout the Christian era there have been other Christians who have rejoiced in the divine glory of Nature, urging their fellows to love and cherish the animals and plants for their own sakes. As early as the second century

Irenaeus, the robust bishop of Lyons, proclaimed that even the tiniest insect is holy, to be treated with reverence. And within the British Isles the early Celtic missionaries are said to have founded monasteries where animals and birds were welcomed as members. Certainly Celtic poetry rings with devotion for every living being. The most famous nature-loving saint was, of course, St Francis, who preached his greatest sermon to the birds.

Today there is a renewal of such vision. We are now terrifyingly aware of the damage that our species is doing in every corner of the globe, endangering and destroying hundreds and thousands of the other species with whom we share this earth. Amidst the campaigns for 'green' politics and economics, many recognize that the radical transformation which is required in our outward pattern of life can only occur if there is a spiritual transformation also. Green politics must be founded on green spirituality – or, to use the more accurate term, 'creation spirituality'. Our hearts and minds must again be captured by that image of paradise contained in the opening pages of the Bible.

The Creation Spirit is a small contribution to this renewal. We have been guided by two principles. The first is that creation spirituality cannot be exclusively religious. Indeed over the centuries secular poets, novelists and essayists have played the greatest part in keeping the creation spirit alive. And the reason for this is important to recognize. The sense of God's spirit infusing every creature is an almost universal human insight; but too frequently wrong-headed doctrines have blinded those who have been trained in Christian theology. So in this collection we juxtapose secular writers with those Christian writers who have shared the same vision.

The second principle is that creation spirituality must at heart be local. We can only glimpse the new Eden if we discover God within the plants and animals all around us. And, acknowledging that each human spirit is formed to the particular culture in which it has been nurtured, we must look first within our own tradition for inspiration. So the writers brought together in this book may broadly be described as belonging to the Celtic and Anglo-Saxon cultures – which, of course, not only embrace the British Isles, but reach across the Atlantic to North America, and onwards across the Pacific to Australasia.

As the titles indicate, the ten chapters take us through the creation story in Genesis. They may, of course, be dipped into at random. But we have designed the book so that it may also be used for meditation, either alone or in a group, or as an aid to worship. For example, each chapter could provide substance for an evening's meditation, reading out some or all of the pieces, interspersed with silence; so the book could be used over ten meetings of a house group. Alternatively a selection of readings from a chapter could be used in place of a sermon at, say, a mid-week Communion service. To help these purposes we begin each chapter with a prayer and end with a hymn.

Any book concerned with creation spirituality must be deeply serious in its interest. After all, it is the survival of God's creatures on this planet which is at stake. But such seriousness does not preclude joy, pleasure and humour. Indeed our hope ultimately rests in humankind finding such joy in Nature, as God created her, that her rape and destruction become utterly repugnant. So this book is, first and foremost, a celebration of creation – to be enjoyed.

I

IN THE BEGINNING

How wonderful and glorious it is to know your love, O God!
Our words cannot express it, nor can our minds describe it.
May we seek to love you with a pure love for your own
sake, and not for what you give us. May our hearts be
touched by the certain knowledge of your presence, and our
minds enlightened by the clear beam of your eternal light.
May we feel and know your beauty and loveliness in ourselves.

THE EPISTLE OF PRAYER (Medieval) adapted

For wisdom is better than rubies; and all things that may be
desired are not to be compared to it. I wisdom dwell with
prudence, and find out knowledge of witty inventions.
    The Lord possessed me in the beginning of his way, before
his works of old. I was set up from everlasting, from the
beginning, or ever the earth was. When there were no depths,
I was brought forth; when there were no fountains abounding
with water. Before the mountains were settled, before the
hills was I brought forth: while as yet he had not made the
earth, nor the fields, nor the highest part of the dust of the
world. When he prepared the heavens, I was there: when he
set a compass upon the face of the depth: when he established
the clouds above: when he strengthened the fountains of the
deep: when he gave to the sea his decree, that the waters
should not pass his commandment: when he appointed the
foundations of the earth: then I was by him, as one brought
up with him: and I was daily his delight, rejoicing always
before him; rejoicing in the habitable part of his earth; and
my delights were with the sons of men.

PROVERBS 8: 11–12, 22–31

In the beginning was the Word, and the Word was with
God, and the Word was God. The same was in the beginning
with God. All things were made by him; and without him
was not any thing made that was made. In him was life.

JOHN 1: 1–4a

1 *The Universe in a Hazelnut*

Our Lord showed me a spiritual sight of his homely and familiar love. I saw that he is everything that is good and comforting to us; he is our clothing – wrapping and enfolding us. He embraces and encloses us in tender love, and he never leaves us. I saw that he is everything that is good, as I understand it.

He showed me a little thing, the size of a hazelnut, lying in the palm of my hand, as round as a ball. I looked at it and thought, 'What can this be?' And I was answered, 'It is all that is made.' I wondered how it could last, for I thought that being so small it might suddenly fall apart. And I was answered in my understanding, 'It lasts, and always will, because God loves it.' And so everything has its being through the love of God.

In this little thing I saw three properties. The first is that God made it; the second is that God loves it; the third is that God preserves it. But what is that to me? It is that God is the creator, the lover and protector. For until I am united to him I cannot know love or rest or true happiness; that is, until I am so at one with him that no created thing can come between my God and me.

JULIAN OF NORWICH *c.* 1342–1420 *Revelations of Divine Love*

2 *On the Universality and Other Attributes of the God of Nature*

All that we see, about, abroad,
What is it all, but nature's God?
In meaner works discovered here
No less than in the starry sphere.

In seas, on earth, this God is seen;
All that exist, upon him lean;
He lives in all, and never strayed
A moment from the works he made.

His system fixed on general laws
Bespeaks a wise creating cause;
Impartially he rules mankind
And all that on this globe we find.

Unchanged in all that seems to change,
Unbounded space is his great range;
To one vast purpose always true,
No time, with him, is old or new.

In all the attributes divine
Unlimited perfectings shine;
In these enwrapt, in these complete,
All virtues in that centre meet.

This power who doth all powers transcend,
To all intelligence a friend,
Exists, the *greatest and the best*
Throughout all worlds, to make them blest.

All that he did he first approved
He all things into *being* loved;
O'er all he made he still presides,
For them in life, or death provides.

PHILIP FRENEAU 1752–1832

3 *I am . . .*

I am the wind that breathes upon the sea,
I am the wave on the ocean,
I am the murmur of leaves rustling,
I am the rays of the sun,
I am the beam of the moon and stars,
I am the power of trees growing,
I am the bud breaking into blossom,
I am the movement of the salmon swimming,
I am the courage of the wild boar fighting,
I am the speed of the stag running,
I am the strength of the ox pulling the plough,
I am the size of the mighty oak tree,
And I am the thoughts of all people
Who praise my beauty and grace.

ANONYMOUS (Celtic)

4 *In the Ears of God*

It is my temper, and I like it the better, to affect all harmony;
and sure there is music even in the beauty and the silent
note which Cupid strikes, far sweeter than the sound of an
instrument. For there is a music wherever there is a harmony, order or proportion: and thus far we may maintain
the music of the spheres; for those well ordered motions and
regular paces, though they give no sound unto the ear, yet
to the understanding they strike a note most full of harmony.
Whosoever is harmonically composed delights in harmony;
which makes me much distrust the symmetry of those heads
which declaim against all church-music. For myself, not only
from my obedience, but my particular genius, I do embrace
it; for even that vulgar and tavern-music, which makes one
man merry, another mad, strikes in me a deep fit of devo-

tion, and a profound contemplation of the first Composer. There is something in it of divinity more than the ear discovers: it is an hieroglyphical and shadowed lesson of the whole world, and creatures of God – such a melody to the ear, as the whole world, well understood, would afford the understanding. In brief, it is a sensible fit of that harmony which intellectually sounds in the ears of God.

THOMAS BROWNE 1605–1682 *Religio Medici*

5 *Harmony to Harmony*

From harmony, from heavenly harmony,
   This universal frame began:
When nature underneath a heap
      Of jarring atoms lay,
      And could not heave her head,
The tuneful voice was heard from high
      'Arise, ye more than dead.'
Then cold, and hot, and moist, and dry
In order to their stations leap,
      And Music's power obey.
From harmony, from heavenly harmony,
      This universal frame began;
      From harmony to harmony
Through all the compass of the notes it ran,
The diapason closing full in man.

JOHN DRYDEN 1631–1700 'Song for St Cecilia's Day'

6 *The Kingdom of God*

O world invisible, we view thee,
O world intangible, we touch thee,
O world unknowable, we know thee,
Inapprehensible, we clutch thee!

Does the fish soar to find the ocean,
The eagle plunge to find the air –
That we ask of the stars in motion
If they have rumour of thee there?

Not where the wheeling systems darken,
And our benumbed conceiving soars! –
The drift of pinions, would we hearken,
Beats at our own clay-shuttered doors.

The angels keep their ancient places; –
Turn but a stone, and start a wing!
'Tis ye, 'tis your estrangèd faces,
That miss the many-splendoured thing.

But (when so sad thou canst not sadder)
Cry; – and upon thy so sore loss
Shall shine the traffic of Jacob's ladder
Pitched betwixt Heaven and Charing Cross.

Yea, in the night, my Soul, my daughter,
Cry, – clinging Heaven by the hems;
And lo, Christ walking on the water
Not of Gennesareth, but Thames!

FRANCIS THOMPSON 1859–1907

7 *In the Garden at Night*

Be still, my soul. Consider
   The flowers and the stars.
Among these sleeping fragrances,
   Sleep now your cares.
That which the universe
   Lacks room to enclose
Lives in the folded petals
   Of this dark rose.

GERALD BULLETT 1893–1958

8 *The World in a Drop of Dew*

The world globes itself in a drop of dew. The microscope
cannot find the animalcule which is less perfect for being
little. Eyes, ears, taste, smell, motion, resistance, appetite,
and organs of reproduction that take hold on eternity, – all
find room to consist in the small creature. So do we put our
life into every act. The true doctrine of omnipresence is that
God reappears with all his parts in every moss and cobweb.
The value of the universe contrives to throw itself into every
point.

RALPH WALDO EMERSON 1803–1882 'Compensation'

9 *The Awful Shadow*

The awful shadow of some unseen Power
   Floats though unseen among us, – visiting
   This various world with as inconstant wing

As summer winds that creep from flower to flower, –
Like moonbeams that behind some piny mountain shower,
    It visits with inconstant grace
    Each human heart and countenance;
Like hues and harmonies of evening, –
    Like clouds in starlight widely spread, –
    Like memory of music fled, –
    Like aught that for its grace may be
Dear, and yet dearer for its mystery.

PERCY BYSSHE SHELLEY 1792–1822
'Hymn to Intellectual Beauty'

10 *The Whole and the Parts*

When in the reason's philosophy the rational appears domi-
nant and sole possessor of the world, we can only wonder
what place would be left to it, if the element excluded might
break through the charm of the magic circle, and, without
growing rational, could find expression. Such an idea may
be senseless, and such a thought may contradict itself, but it
serves to give voice to an obstinate instinct. Unless thought
stands for something that falls beyond mere intelligence, if
'thinking' is not used with some strange implication that
never was part of the meaning of the word, a lingering
scruple still forbids us to believe that reality can ever be
purely rational. It may come from a failure in my metaphys-
ics, or from a weakness of the flesh which continues to
blind me, but the notion that existence could be the same as
understanding strikes as cold and ghost-like as the dreariest
materialism. That the glory of this world in the end is appearance leaves the world more glorious, if we feel it is a show
of some fuller splendour; but the sensuous curtain is a decep-
tion and a cheat, if it hides some colourless movement of
atoms, some spectral woof of impalpable abstractions, or

unearthly ballet of bloodless categories. Though dragged to such conclusions, we cannot embrace them. Our principles may be true, but they are not reality. They no more *make* that Whole which commands our devotion, than some shredded dissection of human tatters is that warm and breathing beauty of flesh which our hearts found delightful.

FRANCIS HERBERT BRADLEY 1846–1924 *The Principles of Logic*

11 *Sweet Contentments*

What sweet contentments doth the soul enjoy by the senses? They are the gates and windows of its knowledge, the organs of its delight. If it be tedious to an excellent player on the lute, to abide but a few months the want of one, how much more must the being without such noble tools and engines be plaintful to the soul? And if two pilgrims which have wandered some few miles together, have a hearts-grief when they are near to part, what must the sorrow be at the parting of two so loving friends and never-loathing lovers as are the body and soul?

WILLIAM DRUMMOND 1585–1649 *A Cypresse Grove*

12 *The Law of Nature*

Now if nature should intermit her course, and leave altogether though it were but for a while the observation of her own laws; if those principal and mother elements of the world, whereof all things in this lower world are made, should lose the qualities which now they have; if the frame of that heavenly arch erected over our heads should loosen and dissolve itself; if celestial spheres should forget their wonted motions, and by irregular volubility turn themselves any way as it might happen; if the prince of the lights of heaven, which now as a giant doth run his unwearied course, should as it were through a languishing faintness begin to stand and to rest himself; if the moon should wander from her beaten way, the times and seasons of the year blend themselves by disordered and confused mixture, the winds breathe out their last gasp, the clouds yield no rain, the earth be defeated of heavenly influence, the fruits of the earth pine away as children at the withered breasts of their mother no longer able to yield them relief: what would become of man himself, whom these things now do all serve? See we not plainly that obedience of creatures unto the law of nature is the stay of the whole world?

RICHARD HOOKER 1554–1600
Of the Laws of Ecclesiastical Politie

13 *Knowledge and Wonder*

If any man shall think by view and inquiry into these sensible and material things to attain that light, whereby he may reveal unto himself the nature or will of God, then indeed is he spoiled by vain philosophy: for the contemplation of God's creatures and works produceth (having regard to the works and creatures themselves) knowledge, but having regard to God, no perfect knowledge, but wonder, which is broken knowledge.

FRANCIS BACON 1561–1626 *The Advancement of Learning*

14 *Cosmic Piety*

There is a philosophic piety which has the universe for its object. This feeling, common to ancient and modern Stoics, has an obvious justification in man's dependence upon the natural world and in its service to many sides of the mind. Such justification of cosmic piety is rather obscured than supported by the euphemisms and ambiguities in which these philosophers usually indulge in their attempt to preserve the customary religious unction. For the more they personify the universe and give it the name of God the more they turn it into a devil. The universe, so far as we can observe it, is a wonderful and immense engine; its extent, its order, its beauty, its cruelty, make it alike impressive. If we dramatize its life and conceive its spirit, we are filled with wonder, terror, and amusement, so magnificent is that spirit, so prolific, inexorable, grammatical, and dull. Like all animals and plants, the cosmos has its own way of doing things, not wholly rational nor ideally best, but patient, fatal, and fruitful. Great is this organism of mud and fire, terrible this vast, painful, glorious experiment. Why should we not look on the universe with piety? Is it not our substance? Are we made of other clay? All our possibilities lie from eternity hidden in its bosom. It is the dispenser of all our joys. We may address it without superstitious terrors; it is not wicked. It follows its own habits abstractedly; it can be trusted to be true to its word. Society is not impossible between it and us, and since it is the source of all our energies, the home of all our happiness, shall we not cling to it and praise it, seeing that it vegetates so grandly and so sadly, and that it is not for us to blame it for what, doubtless, it never knew that it did? Where there is such infinite and laborious potency there is room for every hope.

GEORGE SANTAYANA 1863–1952 *Little Essays*

15 *The Material Becomes Articulate*

Through man alone the material becomes articulate in praise of God. Because man is body he shares in the material world around him, which passes within him through his sense perceptions. Because man is mind he belongs to the world of higher reality and pure spirit. Because he is both, he is, in Cyril of Alexandria's phrase, 'God's crowned image'; he can mould and manipulate the material and render it articulate. The sound in a Byzantine hymn, the gestures in a liturgy, the bricks in a church, the cubes in a mosaic are matter made articulate in the divine praise.

GERVASE MATHEW 1905–1976 *Byzantine Aesthetics*

16 *To See a World*

To see a world in a grain of sand
And a heaven in a wild flower,
Hold infinity in the palm of your hand
And eternity in an hour.

A robin redbreast in a cage
Puts all Heaven in a rage;
A dove-house filled with doves and pigeons
Shudders Hell through all its regions.

WILLIAM BLAKE 1757–1827 'Auguries of Innocence'

17 *Universal Excellency*

God is an universal excellency. All the particular excellencies that are scattered up and down among angels, men, and all other creatures, are virtually and transcendently in him, he hath them all in his own being, Ephes. 1: 3. All creatures in heaven and earth have but their particular excellencies; but God hath in himself the very quintessence of all excellencies. The creatures have but drops of that sea, that ocean, that is in God, they have but their parts of that power, wisdom, goodness, righteousness, holiness, faithfulness, loveliness, desirableness, sweetness, graciousness, beauty, and glory that is in God. One hath this part, and another hath that; one hath this particular excellency, and another hath that; but the whole of all of these parts and excellencies are to be found only in God.

THOMAS BROOKS *d.* 1680 *An Ark for all God's Noahs*

18 *Sanctity in Nature*

Although there was no definite religious sentiment mingled with it, there was a continual perception of Sanctity in the whole of nature, from the slightest thing to the vastest; an instinctive awe, mixed with delight; an indefinable thrill, such as we sometimes imagine to indicate the presence of a disembodied spirit. I could only feel this perfectly when I was alone; and then it would often make me shiver from head to foot with the joy and fear of it, when after being some time away from hills I first got to the shore of a mountain river, where the brown water circled among the pebbles, or when I first saw the swell of distant land against the sunset, or the first low broken wall, covered with mountain moss . . . If we had to explain even the sense of bodily hunger to a person who had never felt it, we should be hard put to it for words; and the joy in nature seemed to me to come of a sort of heart-hunger, satisfied with the presence of a Great and Holy Spirit.

JOHN RUSKIN 1819–1900 *Modern Painters*

19 *Ye Presences of Nature*

Ye Presences of Nature in the sky
And on the earth! Ye Visions of the hills!
And Souls of lonely places! can I think
A vulgar hope was yours when ye employed
Such ministry, when ye, through many a year
Haunting me thus among my boyish sports,
On caves and trees, upon the woods and hills,
Impressed, upon all forms, the characters
Of danger or desire; and thus did make
The surface of the universal earth,
With triumph and delight, with hope and fear,
Work like a sea? . . .

O Soul of Nature! excellent and fair!
That didst rejoice with me, with whom I, too,
Rejoiced through early youth, before the winds
And roaring waters, and the lights and shades
That marched and countermarched about the hills
In glorious apparition, Powers on whom
I daily waited, now all eye and now
All ear; but never long without the heart
Employed, and man's unfolding intellect:
O Soul of Nature! that, by laws divine
Sustained and governed, still dost overflow
With an impassioned life, what feeble ones
Walk on this earth! how feeble have I been
When thou wert in thy strength!

WILLIAM WORDSWORTH 1770–1850 *The Prelude*

20 *The Eye of Providence*

The Word of God is full of the expressions of his love toward man, and all his works do loudly proclaim it. He gave us our being, and by preserving us in it, he renews the donation every moment. He has placed us in a rich and well-furnished world, and has liberally provided for all our necessities. He rains down blessings from Heaven upon us, and causes the earth to bring forth our provision. He gives us our food and raiment, and while we are spending the productions of one year, he is preparing for us against another.

He sweetens our lives with innumerable comforts, and gratifies every faculty with suitable objects. The eye of his Providence is always upon us, and he watches for our safety when we are fast asleep, neither minding him nor ourselves.

But lest we should think these testimonies of his kindness less considerable, because they are the easy issues of his omnipotent power, and do not put him to any trouble or pain, he has taken a more wonderful method to endear himself to us. He has testified his affection to us by suffering as well as by doing; and because he could not suffer in his own nature, he assumed ours.

HENRY SCOUGAL 1650–1678
The Life of God in the Soul of Man

Hymn: O Praise ye the Lord!

O Praise ye the Lord!
  Praise him in the height;
Rejoice in his word,
  Ye angels of light;
Ye heavens, adore him,
  By whom ye were made,
And worship before him,
  In brightness arrayed.

O praise ye the Lord!
  Praise him upon earth,
In tuneful accord,
  Ye sons of new birth.
Praise him who hath brought you
  His grace from above,
Praise him who hath taught you
  To sing of his love.

O praise ye the Lord!
  All things that give sound;
Each jubilant chord
  Re-echo around;
Loud organs his glory
  Forth tell in deep tone,
And, sweet harp, the story
  Of what he hath done.

O praise ye the Lord!
  Thanksgiving and song
To him be outpoured
  All ages along;
For love in creation,
  For heavens restored,
For grace of salvation,
  O praise ye the Lord!

HENRY WILLIAMS BAKER 1821–1877

2

GOD CREATED HEAVEN AND EARTH

Lead us, O God, from the sight of the lovely things of the world to the thought of thee their Creator; and grant that delighting in the beautiful things of thy creation we may delight in thee, the first author of beauty and the Sovereign Lord of all thy works, blessed for evermore.

GEORGE APPLETON *b.* 1902

O Lord, how manifold are thy works! in wisdom hast thou made them all: the earth is full of thy riches. So is this great and wide sea, wherein are things creeping innumerable, both small and great beasts. There go the ships: there is that leviathan, whom thou hast made to play therein. These wait all upon thee; that thou mayest give them their meat in due season. That thou givest them they gather: thou openest thine hand, they are filled with good. Thou hidest thy face, they are troubled: thou takest away their breath, they die, and return to their dust. Thou sendest forth thy spirit, they are created: and thou renewest the face of the earth. The glory of the Lord shall endure for ever: the Lord shall rejoice in his works.

PSALM 104: 24–31

Through faith we understand that the worlds were framed by the word of God, so that things which are seen were not made of things which do appear.

HEBREWS 11: 3

1 *Creation*

Eternal is the creator who rules this earth,
Whose sustaining power governs this world.
Mighty is the monarch who is king and master over all;
He rules and guides both earth and heaven,
Even as he encompasses them.
He created me in the beginning when he first established
       this earth;
He ordained that I should stay awake and never sleep again.
The almighty creator guides this earth with his power,
So that by his word I embrace the whole world.
I am so timid that a swift-moving spectre can terrify me;
And yet I am as bold as a wild boar,
Which stands at bay, enraged with fury.
No warrior on earth can overcome me,
But only God who governs and rules this high heaven.

ANONYMOUS *c.* 850 'Riddles' from *The Exeter Book*

2 *King of the World*

My dear King, my own King, without pride, without sin, you created the whole world, eternal, victorious King.

King above the elements, King above the sun, King beneath the ocean, King of the north and south, the east and west, against you no enemy can prevail.

King of the Mysteries, you existed before the elements, before the sun was set in the sky, before the waters covered the ocean floor; beautiful King, you are without beginning and without end.

King, you created the daylight, and made the darkness; you are not arrogant or boastful, and yet strong and firm.

King, you created the land out of shapeless mass, you carved the mountains and chiselled the valleys, and covered the earth with trees and grass.

King, you stretched out the sky above the earth, a perfect sphere like a perfect apple, and you decorated the sky with stars to shine at night.

King, you pierced the earth with springs from which pure water flows, to form streams and rivers across the land.

King, you ordained the eight winds, the four primary winds from north and south, east and west, and the four lesser winds that swirl hither and thither.

You gave each wind its own colour: the north wind is white, bringing snow in winter; the south wind is red, carrying warmth in summer; the west wind is blue, a cooling breeze across the sea; the east wind is yellow, scorching in summer and bitter in winter; and the lesser winds are green, orange, purple and black – the black wind that blows in the darkest nights.

King, you measured each object and each span within the universe: the heights of the mountains and the depths of the oceans; the distance from the sun to the moon, and from star to star.

You ordained the movements of every object: the sun to cross the sky each day, and the moon to rise each night; the clouds to carry rain from the sea, and the rivers to carry water back from the sea.

King, you divided the earth into three zones: the north cold and bitter; the south hot and dry; and the middle zone cool, wet and fertile.

And you created men and women to be your stewards of the earth, always praising you for your boundless love.

OENGUS THE CULDEE (9th century) attributed *The Celtic Psalter*

3 *Children of Men*

Children of men, lift up your hearts. Laud and magnify God, the everlasting Wisdom, the holy, undivided and adorable Trinity.

Praise him that he hath made man in his own image, a maker and craftsman like himself, a little mirror of his triune majesty.

For every work of creation is threefold, an earthly trinity to match the heavenly.

First: there is the Creative Idea; passionless, timeless, beholding the whole work complete at once, the end in the beginning; and this is the image of the Father.

Second: there is the Creative Energy, begotten of that Idea, working in time from the beginning to the end, with sweat and passion, being incarnate in the bonds of matter; and this is the image of the Word.

Third: there is the Creative Power, the meaning of the work and its response in the lively soul; and this is the image of the indwelling Spirit.

And these three are one, each equally in itself the whole work, whereof none can exist without other; and this is the image of the Trinity.

DOROTHY L. SAYERS 1893–1957 *The Zeal of thy House*

4 *An Ingenious Formation*

That the universe was formed by a fortuitous concourse of atoms, I will no more believe than that the accidental jumbling of the alphabet would fall into a most ingenious treatise of philosophy.

JONATHAN SWIFT 1667–1745

5 *The Mirror of God*

There is not so poor a creature but may be thy glass to see God in. The greatest flat glass that can be made cannot represent any thing greater than it is. If every gnat that flies were an Archangel, all that could but tell me, that there is a God; and the poorest worm that creeps tells me that. If I should ask the basilisk, how camest thou by those killing eyes, he would tell me, thy God made me so; and if I should ask the slow-worm how camest thou to be without eyes, he would tell me, thy God made me so. The cedar is no better a glass to see God in, than the hyssop on the wall; all things that are, are equally removed from being nothing; and what-soever hath any being, is by that very being a glass in which we see God, who is the root, and the fountain of all being. The whole frame of nature is the theatre, the whole volume of creatures is the glass, and the light of nature, reason, is our light.

JOHN DONNE 1572–1631
'Preached at St Paul's, in the Evening,
upon Easter Day. 1625'

6 *Partaking of His Nature*

God created everything to partake of his own nature, to have some degree and share of his own life and happiness. Nothing can be good or evil, happy or unhappy, but as it does or does not stand in the same degree of divine life in which it was created, receiving in God and from God all that good that it is capable of, and co-operating with him according to the nature of its powers and perfections.

WILLIAM LAW 1686–1761
An Earnest and Serious Answer to Dr Trapp

7 *An Infusion of Bliss*

It is, as sometimes in nature, when every breath of wind is so lulled asleep that not a leaf moves on the bough of any tree; the sun is shedding his parting ray on the still foliage; and the sea rests as if it had become a pavement of crystal. This is peace in nature. Your heart feels, amid such a scene, not only the absence of whatsoever might create alarm or disquiet, but the presence of some elements of positive enjoyment, as if there were an infusion of bliss in the scene. Now it is infinitely more so in the kingdom of grace.

ANDREW A. BONAR 1810–1892
The Gospel Pointing to the Person of Christ

8 *Hidden Joys*

Pleasures lie thickest where no pleasures seem;
There's not a leaf that falls upon the ground
But holds some joy, of silence or of sound,
Some sprite begotten of a summer dream.
The very meanest things are made supreme
With innate ecstasy. No grain of sand
But moves a bright and million-peopled land,
And hath its Edens and its Eves, I deem.
For Love, though blind himself, a curious eye
Hath lent me, to behold the heart of things,
And touched mine ear with power. Thus far or nigh,
Minute or mighty, fixed or free with wings,
Delight from many a nameless covert sly
Peeps sparkling, and in tones familiar sings.

SAMUEL LAMAN BLANCHARD 1804–1845

9 *Miracles*

Why, who makes much of a miracle?
As to me I know of nothing else but miracles,
Whether I walk the streets of Manhattan,
Or dart my sight over the roofs of houses towards the sky,
Or wade with naked feet along the beach just in the edge
     of the water,
Or stand under trees in the woods,
Or talk by day with any one I love, or sleep in the bed at
     night with any one I love,
Or sit at table at dinner with the rest,
Or look at strangers opposite me riding in the car,
Or watch honey-bees busy around the hive of a summer
     fore-noon,
Or animals feeding in the fields,
Or birds, or the wonderfulness of insects in the air,
Or the wonderfulness of the sundown, or of stars shining
     so quiet and bright,
Or the exquisite delicate thin curve of the new moon in
     spring;
These with the rest, one and all, are to me miracles,
The whole referring, yet each distinct and in its place.

To me every hour of the light and dark is a miracle,
Every cubic inch of space is a miracle,
Every square yard of the surface of the earth is spread with
     the same,
Every foot of the interior swarms with the same.

To me the sea is a continual miracle,
The fishes that swim – the rocks – the motion of the waves
     – the ships with men in them,
What stranger miracles are there?

WALT WHITMAN 1819–1892

10 *The Glory of the Garden*

There's not a pair of legs so thin, there's not a head so
        thick,
There's not a hand so weak and white, nor yet a heart so
        sick,
But it can find some needful job that's crying to be done,
For the Glory of the Garden glorifieth every one.

Then seek your job with thankfulness and work till further
        orders,
If it's only netting strawberries or killing slugs on borders;
And when your back stops aching and your hands begin
        to harden,
You will find yourself a partner in the Glory of the Garden.

Oh, Adam was a gardener, and God who made him sees
That half a proper gardener's work is done upon his knees,
So when your work is finished, you can wash your hands
        and pray
For the Glory of the Garden that it may not pass away!
And the Glory of the Garden it shall never pass away!

                            RUDYARD KIPLING 1865–1936

11 *I Never Saw a Moor*

I never saw a Moor –
I never saw the Sea –
Yet know I how the Heather looks
And what a Billow be.

I never spoke with God
Nor visited in Heaven –
Yet certain am I of the spot
As if the Checks were given –

                        EMILY DICKINSON 1830–1886

12 *A Small Display*

First, Canst thou by *searching* find out God? Yes. Because, in the first place, I know I did not make myself, and yet I have existence; and by *searching* into the nature of other things, I find that no other thing could make itself; and yet millions of other things exist; therefore it is, that I know, by positive conclusion resulting from this search, that there is a power superior to all those things, and that power is God.

Secondly, Canst thou find out the Almighty to *perfection*? No. Not only because the power and wisdom he has manifested in the structure of the Creation that I behold is to me incomprehensible; but because even this manifestation, great as it is, is probably but a small display of that immensity of power and wisdom, by which millions of other worlds, to me invisible by their distance, were created and continue to exist.

THOMAS PAINE 1737–1809 *The Age of Reason*

13 *Religious Feeling*

You will hardly find one among the profounder sort of scientific minds without a religious feeling of his own. But it is different from the religiosity of the naïve man. For the latter, God is a being from whose care one hopes to benefit and whose punishment one fears; a sublimation of a feeling similar to that of a child for its father, a being to whom one stands, so to speak, in a personal relation, however deeply it may be tinged with awe.

But the scientist is possessed by the sense of universal causation. The future, to him, is every whit as necessary and determined as the past. There is nothing divine about morality; it is a purely human affair. His religious feeling takes the form of a rapturous amazement at the harmony of natural law, which reveals an intelligence of such superiority that, compared with it, all the systematic thinking and acting of human beings is an utterly insignificant reflection. This feeling is the guiding principle of his life and work, in so far as he succeeds in keeping himself from the shackles of selfish desire. It is beyond question closely akin to that which has possessed the religious geniuses of all ages.

ALBERT EINSTEIN 1879–1955 *Ideas and Opinions*

14 *God in the World*

God is *in* the world, or nowhere, creating continually in us and around us. This creative principle is everywhere, in animate and so-called inanimate matter, in the ether, water, earth, human hearts. But this creation is a continuing process, and 'the process is itself the actuality,' since no sooner do you arrive than you start on a fresh journey. In so far as man partakes of this creative process does he partake of the divine, of God, and that participation is his immortality, reducing the question of whether his individuality survives death of the body to the estate of an irrelevancy. His true destiny as co-creator in the universe is his dignity and his grandeur.

ALFRED NORTH WHITEHEAD 1861–1947
Dialogues of Alfred North Whitehead

15 *Continuous Creation*

Although I think there is no doubt that every galaxy we observe to be receding from us will in about 100,000,000,000 years, have passed entirely beyond the limit of vision of an observer in our Galaxy, yet I think that such an observer would still be able to see about the same number of galaxies as we do now. By this I mean that new galaxies will have condensed out of the background material at just about the rate necessary to compensate for those that are being lost as a consequence of their passing beyond our observable Universe. At first sight it might be thought that this could not go on indefinitely because the material forming the background would ultimately become exhausted. The reason why this is not so, is that new material appears in space to compensate for the background material that is constantly being condensed into galaxies. This is, perhaps, the most surprising of all the conceptions described in this book. For I find myself forced to assume that the nature of the Universe requires continuous creation – the perpetual bringing into being of new background material . . .

The most obvious question to ask about continuous creation is this: Where does the created material come from? At one time created atoms do not exist, at a later time they do. The creation arises from a field, which you must think of as generated by the matter that exists already. We are well used to the idea of matter giving rise to a gravitational field. Now we must think of it also giving rise to a creation field. Matter that already exists causes new matter to appear. Matter chases its own tail. This may seem a very strange idea and I agree that it is, but in science it does not matter how strange an idea may seem so long as it works – that is to say, so long as the idea can be expressed in a precise form, and so long as its consequences are found to be in agreement with observation.

FRED HOYLE *b.* 1915 *The Nature of the Universe*

16 *The Author and Giver*

All science has God as its author and giver. Much is heard of the conflict between science and religion, and of the contrast between sacred and secular. There may be aspects of truth to which religion is the gate, as indeed there are aspects of truth to which particular sciences are the gate. But if there be a Creator, and if truth be one of his attributes, then everything that is true can claim his authorship, and every search for truth can claim his authority.

When science has appeared to be anti-religious it generally has meant that one or two particular sciences were exaggerating their claim to a sort of omnicompetence for reading the whole meaning of the universe, even though one particular science is, of course, not competent to do more than read one particular aspect of the universe. But the more we Christians are ready to see and acknowledge God in the sciences – God in the truly scientific spirit – the more we shall be witnessing to what is true to the presence of God in the world, and the more entitled we shall be to go on to point out that there can indeed be a certain sort of scientifically trained mentality which is narrow and unperceptive, and robbing itself of a real chance of interpreting the universe aright.

MICHAEL RAMSEY 1904–1988
Through the Year with Michael Ramsey

17 *His Volition*

The essence of the doctrine of Creation is not that God inaugurated the existence of the world at a particular moment of time, but that it owes its existence – not only its beginning – to his volitional activity.

WILLIAM TEMPLE 1881–1944 *Nature, Man and God*

18 *The Year's at the Spring*

The year's at the spring
And day's at the morn;
Morning's at seven;
The hill-side's dew-pearled;
The lark's on the wing;
The snail's on the thorn:
God's in his heaven –
All's right with the world!

ROBERT BROWNING 1812–1889 'Pippa Passes'

19 *The Beauty of the World*

It's only now I am beginning to see again and to recognize
again the beauty of the world. Take the swallows to-day,
their flutter-flutter, their velvet-forked tails, their transparent
wings that are like the fins of fishes. The little dark head and
breast golden in the light. Then the beauty of the garden,
and the beauty of raked paths . . . Then, the silence.

KATHERINE MANSFIELD 1888–1923 *Journal*

20 *The Marriage of the Soul*

Nature will bear the closest inspection. She invites us to lay
our eye level with her smallest leaf, and take an insect view
of its plain . . .
    It is the marriage of the soul with Nature that makes the
intellect fruitful, and gives birth to imagination . . .
    We soon get through with Nature. She excites an expec-
tation which she cannot satisfy. The merest child which has

rambled into a copsewood dreams of a wildness so wild and
strange and inexhaustible as Nature can never show him.

HENRY DAVID THOREAU 1817–1862 *Journal*

Hymn: O Worship the King

O worship the King, all glorious above;
O gratefully sing his power and his love:
Our shield and defender, the ancient of days,
Pavilioned with splendour, and girded with praise.

O tell of his might, O sing of his grace,
Whose robe is the light, whose canopy space.
His chariots of wrath, the deep thunder-clouds form,
And dark is his path on the wings of the storm.

This earth, with its store of wonders untold,
Almighty, thy power hath founded of old;
Hath stablished it fast by a changeless decree,
And round it hath cast, like a mantle, the sea.

Thy bountiful care what tongue can recite?
It breathes in the air, it shines in the light;
It streams from the hills, it descends to the plain,
And sweetly distils in the dew and the rain.

O measureless might, ineffable love,
While angels delight to hymn thee above,
Thy humbler creation, though feeble their lays,
With true adoration shall sing to thy praise.

ROBERT GRANT 1779–1838

3

LET THERE BE LIGHT

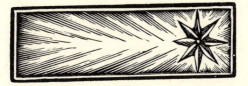

Blessed art thou, O Lord, who madest the two lights, sun and moon, the greater and the lesser, and the stars for lights, for signs, for seasons, spring, summer, autumn, winter, days, weeks, months, years, to rule over day and night.

Glory be to thee, O Lord, for that thou didst create not only the visible light, but the light invisible, that which may be known of God, the law written in the heart.

LANCELOT ANDREWES 1555–1626

To whom then will ye liken me, or shall I be equal? saith the Holy One. Lift up your eyes on high, and behold who hath created these things, that bringeth out their host by number: he calleth them all by names by the greatness of his might, for that he is strong in power; not one faileth.

ISAIAH 40: 25–26

This then is the message which we have heard of him, and declare unto you, that God is light, and in him is no darkness at all. If we say that we have fellowship with him, and walk in darkness, we lie, and do not the truth: but if we walk in the light, as he is in the light, we have fellowship one with another, and the blood of Jesus Christ his Son cleanseth us from all sin.

I JOHN I: 5–7

1 *Inward Sweetness*

Not long after I first began to experience these things, I gave an account to my father of some things that had passed in my mind. I was pretty much affected by the discourse we had together; and when the discourse was ended, I walked abroad alone, in a solitary place in my father's pasture, for contemplation. And as I was walking there, and looking up on the sky and clouds, there came into my mind so sweet a sense of the glorious *majesty* and *grace* of God, that I know not how to express. I seemed to see them both in a sweet conjunction; majesty and meekness joined together; it was a sweet, and gentle, and holy majesty; and also a majestic meekness; an awful sweetness; a high, and great, and holy gentleness.

After this my sense of divine things gradually increased, and became more and more lively, and had more of that inward sweetness. The appearance of every thing was altered; there seemed to be, as it were, a calm, sweet cast, or appearance of divine glory, in almost every thing. God's excellency, his wisdom, his purity and love, seemed to appear in every thing; in the sun, moon, and stars; in the clouds, and blue sky; in the grass, flowers, trees; in the water, and all nature; which used greatly to fix my mind. I often used to sit and view the moon for continuance; and in the day, spent much time in viewing the clouds and sky, to behold the sweet glory of God in these things; in the mean time, singing forth, with a low voice my contemplations of the Creator and Redeemer. And scarce any thing, among all the works of nature, was so sweet to me as thunder and lightning; formerly, nothing had been so terrible to me. Before, I used to be uncommonly terrified with thunder, and to be struck with terror when I saw a thunder storm rising; but now, on the contrary, it rejoiced me. I felt God, so to speak, at the first appearance of a thunder storm; and used to take the opportunity, at such times, to fix myself in order to view the clouds, and see the lightnings play, and hear the majestic and awful voice of God's thunder, which oftentimes was exceedingly entertaining, leading me to sweet contemplations of my great and glorious God.

JONATHAN EDWARDS 1703–1758 *Personal Narrative*

2 *Pure Light*

There are days now and again when the summer broods in Trafalgar Square; the flood of light from a cloudless sky gathers and grows, thickening the air; the houses enclose the beams as water is enclosed in a cup. Sideways from the white-painted walls light is reflected; upwards from the broad, heated pavement in the centre light and heat ascend; from the blue heaven it presses downwards. Not only from the sun – one point – but from the entire width of the visible blue the brilliant stream flows. Summer is enclosed between the banks of houses – all summer's glow and glory of exceeding brightness. The blue panel overhead has but a stray fleck of cloud, a Cupid drawn on the panel in pure white, but made indefinite by distance. The joyous swallows climb high into the illuminated air till the eye, daunted by the glow, can scarce detect their white breasts as they turn . . .

Either the light subdues the sound, or perhaps rather it renders the senses slumberous and less sensitive, but the great sunlit square is silent – silent, that is, for the largest city on earth. A slumberous silence of abundant light, of the full summer day, of the high flood of summer hours whose tide can rise no higher. A time to linger and dream under the beautiful breast of heaven, heaven brooding and descending in pure light upon man's handiwork. If the light shall thus come in, and of its mere loveliness overcome every aspect of dreariness, why shall not the light of thought, and hope – the light of the soul – overcome and sweep away the dust of our lives?

RICHARD JEFFERIES 1848–1887 *The Life of the Fields*

3 *Dancing*

Dancing, bright lady, then began to be,
  When the first seeds whereof the world did spring,
The fire, air, earth, and water, did agree
  By Love's persuasion, nature's mighty king,
  To leave their first discorded combating,
    And in a dance such measure to observe,
    As all the world their motion should preserve.

Since when they still are carried in a round,
  And changing come one in another's place;
Yet do they neither mingle nor confound,
  But every one doth keep the bounded space
  Wherein the dance doth bid it turn or trace.
    This wondrous miracle did Love devise,
    For dancing is love's proper exercise.

Like this he framed the god's eternal bower,
  And of a shapeless and confusèd mass,
By his through-piercing and digesting power,
  The turning vault of heaven formèd was,
  Whose starry wheels he hath so made to pass,
    As that their movings do a music frame,
    And they themselves still dance unto the same.

For that brave sun, the father of the day,
  Doth love this earth, the mother of the night;
And, like a reveller in rich array,
  Doth dance his galliard in his leman's sight,
  Both back and forth and sideways passing light.
    His gallant grace doth so the gods amaze,
    That all stand still and at his beauty gaze.

JOHN DAVIES 1569–1626 'The Praise of Dancing'

4 *Easter Sunday*

The people say that the sun dances on this day in joy for a risen Saviour.

Old Barbara Macphie at Dreimsdale saw this once, but only once, during her long life. And the good woman, of high natural intelligence, described in poetic language and with religious fervour what she saw or believed she saw from the summit of Benmore:

'The glorious gold-bright sun was after rising on the crests of the great hills, and it was changing colour – green, purple, red, blood-red, white, intense-white, and gold-white, like the glory of the God of the elements to the children of men. It was dancing up and down in exultation at the joyous resurrection of the beloved Saviour of victory.

'To be thus privileged, a person must ascend to the top of the highest hill before sunrise, and believe that the God who makes the small blade of grass to grow is the same God who makes the large, massive sun to move.'

ALEXANDER CARMICHAEL 1832–1912, *Carmina Gadelica*

5 *Dies Dominica!*

Dies Dominica! the sunshine burns
strong incense on the breathing fields of morn:
lucid, intense, all colour towards it yearns
that souls of flowers on the air are born.

What claustral joy to-day is on the air
– expanding now and one with the celebrant sun –
and fills with pointed flame all things aware,
all flowers and souls that sing – and I am one!

Dies Dominica! the passion yearns,
and the whole world and singer is but one flower
from out whose luminous chalice odour burns
intenser toward the blue thro' this keen hour:

– this hour is my eternity! the soul
rises, expanding ever, with the sight,
thro' flowers and colours, and the visible whole
of beauty mingled in one dream of light.

CHRISTOPHER BRENNAN 1870–1932

6 *What Links are Ours*

What links are ours with orbs that are
   So resolutely far:
The solitary asks, and they
Give radiance as from a shield:
   Still at the death of day,
   The seen, the unrevealed.
   Implacable they shine
To us who would of Life obtain
An answer for the life we strain
   To nourish with one sign.
Nor can imagination throw
The penetrative shaft: we pass
The breath of thought, who would divine
   If haply they may grow
As Earth; have our desire to know;
If life comes there to grain from grass;
And flowers like ours of toil and pain;
   Has passion to beat bar,
   Win space from cleaving brain;
   The mystic link attain,
   Whereby star holds on star . . .

Let it but be the lord of Mind to guide
Our eyes; no branch of Reason's growing lopped;
Nor dreaming on a dream; but fortified
By day to penetrate black midnight; see,
Hear, feel, outside the senses; even that we,
The specks of dust upon a mound of mould,
We who reflect those rays, though low our place,
    To them are lastingly allied.

So may we read, and little find them cold:
Not frosty lamps illumining dead space,
Not distant aliens, not senseless Powers.
The fire is in them whereof we are born;
The music of their motion may be ours.
Spirit shall deem them beckoning Earth and voiced
Sisterly to her, in her beams rejoiced.
Of love, the grand impulsion, we behold
    The love that lends her grace
    Among the starry fold.
Then at new flood of customary morn,
    Look at her through her showers,
    Her mists, her streaming gold,
A wonder edges the familiar face:
She wears no more the robe of printed hours;
Half strange seems Earth, and sweeter than her flowers.

GEORGE MEREDITH 1828–1909 'Meditation under Stars'

7 *An Hymn to Evening*

Soon as the sun forsook the eastern main
The pealing thunder shook the heav'nly plain;
Majestic grandeur! From the Zephyr's wing,
Exhales the incense of the blooming spring.
Soft purl the streams, the birds renew their notes,
And through the air their mingled music floats.

Through all the heav'ns what beauteous dyes are spread!
But the west glories in the deepest red:
So may our breasts with ev'ry virtue glow,
The living temples of our God below!

Filled with the praise of him who gives the light;
And draws the sable curtains of the night,
Let placid slumbers soothe each weary mind,
At morn to wake more heav'nly, more refined;
So shall the labours of the day begin
More pure, more guarded from the snares of sin.

Night's leaden sceptre seals my drowsy eyes,
Then cease, my song, till fair *Aurora* rise.

PHILLIS WHEATLEY *c.* 1754–1784

8 *All Other Love is Like The Moon*

All other love is like the moon
That waxeth or waneth as flower in plain,
As flower that blooms and fadeth soon,
As day that showereth and ends in rain.

All other love begins with bliss,
In weeping and woe makes its ending;
No love there is that's our whole bliss
But that which rests on heaven's king.

ANONYMOUS *c.* 1350 'Love True and Ever Green'

9 *How Sweet the Moonlight*

How sweet the moonlight sleeps upon this bank!
Here will we sit, and let the sounds of music
Creep in our ears: soft stillness and the night
Become the touches of sweet harmony:

Sit, Jessica; look how the floor of heaven
Is thick inlaid with patines of bright gold.
There's not the smallest orb which thou behold'st
But in his motion like an angel sings,
Still choiring to the young-eyed cherubims;
Such harmony is in immortal souls;
But whilst this muddy vesture of decay
Doth grossly close it in, we cannot hear it.

WILLIAM SHAKESPEARE 1564–1616 *The Merchant of Venice*

10 *Lady Moon*

Lady Moon, Lady Moon, where are you roving?
    Over the sea.
Lady Moon, Lady Moon, whom are you loving?
    All that love me.

Are you not tired with rolling, and never
    Resting to sleep?
Why look so pale, and so sad, as for ever
    Wishing to weep?

Ask me not this, little child, if you love me;
    You are too bold;
I must obey my dear Father above me,
    And do as I'm told.

Lady Moon, Lady Moon, where are you roving?
    Over the sea.
Lady Moon, Lady Moon, whom are you loving?
    All that love me.

RICHARD MONCKTON MILNES 1809–1885

11 *I Saw Eternity*

I saw eternity the other night
Like a great ring of pure and endless light,
    All calm, as it was bright;
And, round beneath it, time, in hours, days, years,
    Driven by the spheres,
Like a vast shadow moved, in which the world
    And all her train were hurled.

HENRY VAUGHAN 1621–1695 'The World'

12 *Lie on the Grass at Night*

'I don't know about ghosts,' she was saying; 'but I do know that our souls can be made to go outside our bodies when we are alive.'

The dairyman turned to her with his mouth full, his eyes charged with serious inquiry, and his great knife and fork (breakfasts were breakfasts here) planted erect on the table, like the beginning of a gallows.

'What – really now? And is it so, maidy?' he said.

'A very easy way to feel 'em go,' continued Tess, 'is to lie on the grass at night and look straight up at some big bright star; and, by fixing your mind upon it, you will soon find that you are hundreds and hundreds o' miles away from your body, which you don't seem to want at all.'

The dairyman removed his hard gaze from Tess, and fixed it on his wife.

'Now that's a rum thing, Christianner – hey? To think o' the miles I've vamped o' starlight nights these last thirty year, courting, or trading, or for doctor, or for nurse, and yet never had the least notion o' that till now, or feeled my soul rise so much as an inch above my shirt-collar.'

The general attention being drawn to her, including that of the dairyman's pupil, Tess flushed, and remarking evasively that it was only a fancy, resumed her breakfast.

THOMAS HARDY 1840–1928 *Tess of the d'Urbervilles*

13 *Organs of Divine Providence*

And certainly it cannot be doubted but the stars are instruments of a far greater use than to give an obscure light, and for men to gaze on after sunset: it being manifest that the diversity of seasons, the winters and summers, more hot and cold, are not so uncertained by the sun and moon alone, who alway keep one and the same course; but that the stars have also their working therein.

And if we cannot deny, but that God hath given virtue to springs and fountains, to cold earth, to plants and stones, minerals, and to the excremental parts of the basest living creatures, why should we rob the beautiful stars of their working powers? For, seeing they are many in number, and of eminent beauty and magnitude, we may not think that in the treasury of his wisdom who is infinite, there can be wanting, even for every star, a peculiar virtue and operation; as every herb, plant, fruit, and flower adorning the face of the earth hath the like. For as these were not created to beautify the earth alone, and to cover and shadow her dusty face, but otherwise for the use of man and beast, to feed them and cure them, so were not those uncountable glorious bodies set in the firmament to no other end than to adorn it, but for instruments and organs of his divine providence so far as it hath pleased his just will to determine.

WALTER RALEIGH *c.* 1552–1618 *History of the World*

14 *An Ode*

The spacious firmament on high
With all the blue ethereal sky,
And spangled heavens, a shining frame,
Their great original proclaim:
The unwearied sun, from day to day,
Does his Creator's power display,
And publishes to every land
The work of an Almighty hand.

Soon as the evening shades prevail,
The moon takes up the wondrous tale,
And nightly to the listening earth
Repeats the story of her birth;
Whilst all the stars that round her burn,
And all the planets in their turn,
Confirm the tidings as they roll,
And spread the truth from pole to pole.

What though, in solemn silence, all
Move round the dark, terrestrial ball?
What though, no real voice, nor sound,
Amidst their radiant orbs be found?
In reason's ear they all rejoice,
And utter forth a glorious voice,
For ever singing, as they shine,
'The hand that made us is divine'.

JOSEPH ADDISON 1672–1719

15 *Raise Now Your Thoughts*

Raise now your thoughts from this ball of earth to all those glorious luminaries that adorn the high arch of heaven. The motion and situation of the planets, are they not admirable for use and order? Were those (miscalled *erratique*) globes once known to stray, in their repeated journeys through the pathless void? Do they not measure areas round the sun, ever proportioned to the times? So fixed, so immutable are the laws by which the unseen Author of Nature actuates the universe. How vivid and radiant is the lustre of the fixed stars! How magnificent and rich that negligent profusion with which they appear to be scattered through the whole azure vault! Yet, if you take the telescope, it brings into your view a new host of stars that escape the naked eye. Here they seem contiguous and minute, but, to a nearer view, immense orbs of light at various distances far sunk in the abyss of space. Now you must call imagination to your aid: the feeble, narrow sense cannot descry innumerable worlds revolving round the central fires, and, in those worlds, the energy of an all-perfect mind displayed in endless forms. But neither sense nor imagination are big enough to comprehend the boundless extent, with all its dazzling furniture. Though the labouring mind exert and strain each power to its utmost reach, there still stands out ungrasped a surplusage immeasurable. Yet all the vast bodies that compose this mighty frame, how distant and remote soever, are, by some secret mechanism, some divine art and force, linked in a mutual dependence and intercourse with each other, even with this earth, which almost slipped from my thoughts, and was lost in the crowd of worlds. Is not the whole system immense, beautiful, glorious beyond expression and beyond thought? What treatment then do those Philosophers deserve, who would deprive these noble and delightful

scenes of all reality? How should those principles be enter-
tained, that lead us to think all the visible beauty of the
creation a false imaginary glare?

GEORGE BERKELEY 1685–1753 *Dialogues*

16 *There is a Spot*

There is a spot, 'mid barren hills,
　Where winter howls, and driving rain;
But if the dreary tempest chills,
　There is a light that warms again.

The house is old, the trees are bare,
　Moonless above bends twilight's dome;
But what on earth is half so dear –
　So longed for – as the hearth of home?

The mute bird sitting on the stone,
　The dank moss dripping from the wall,
The thorn-trees gaunt, the walks o'ergrown,
　I love them – how I love them all! . . .

A little and a lone green lane
　That opened on a common wide;
A distant, dreamy, dim blue chain
　Of mountains circling every side.

A heaven so clear, an earth so calm,
　So sweet, so soft, so hushed an air;
And, deepening still the dream-like charm,
　Wild moor-sheep feeding everywhere.

EMILY BRONTË 1818–1848 'A Little While'

17 *Knowledge of the Wind*

The wind is sometimes plain up and down, which is commonly most certain, and requireth least knowledge, wherein a mean shooter with mean gear, if he can shoot home, may make best shift. A side wind trieth an archer and good gear very much. Sometime it bloweth aloft, sometime hard by the ground; sometime it bloweth by blasts, and sometime it continueth all in one; sometime full side wind, sometime quarter with him and more, and likewise against him, as a man with casting up light grass, or else if he take good heed, shall sensibly learn by experience. To see the wind, with a man his eyes, it is impossible, the nature of it is so fine and subtle . . .

And that which was the most marvel of all, at one time two drifts of snow flew, the one out of the west into the east, the other out of the north into the east: and I saw two winds by reason of the snow, the one cross over the other, as it had been two highways. And again, I should hear the wind blow in the air, when nothing was stirred at the ground. And when all was still where I rode, not very far from me the snow should be lifted wonderfully. This experience made me more marvel at the nature of the wind, than it made me cunning in the knowledge of the wind.

ROGER ASCHAM 1515–1568 *Toxophilus*

18 *The Weather's Pledge*

After a debauch of thunder-shower, the weather takes the pledge and signs it with a rainbow.

THOMAS BAILEY ALDRICH 1836–1907 *Ponkapog Papers*

19 *The Gem-like Flame*

Every moment some form grows perfect in hand or face; some tone on the hills or sea is choicer than the rest; some mood of passion or insight or intellectual excitement is irresistibly real and attractive for us, – for that moment only. Not the fruit of experience, but experience itself is the end. A counted number of pulses only is given to us of a variegated, dramatic life. How may we see in them all that is to be seen in them by the finest senses? How can we pass most swiftly from point to point, and be present always at the focus where the greatest number of vital forces unite in their purest energy?

To burn always with this hard gem-like flame, to maintain this ecstasy, is success in life . . . While all melts under our feet, we may well catch at any exquisite passion, or any contribution to knowledge that seems, by a lifted horizon, to set the spirit free for a moment, or any stirring of the senses, strange dyes, strange flowers, and curious odours, or work of the artist's hands, or the face of one's friend. Not to discriminate every moment some passionate attitude in those about us, and in the brilliance of their gifts some tragic dividing of forces on their ways is, on this short day of frost and sun, to sleep before evening.

WALTER PATER 1839–1894
Studies in the History of the Renaissance

20 *We are Small Enough*

William Beebee, the naturalist, tells of a ritual through which he and the late President Roosevelt used to go. After an evening chat they would step outside and look up at the heavens. Searching with or without the aid of glasses until they found the faint spot of light-mist below the lower left-hand corner of the great square of Pegasus, one of them would recite: 'That is the Spiral Galaxy of Andromeda. It is as large as our Milky Way. It is one of a hundred million galaxies. It is seven hundred and fifty thousand light years away. It consists of one hundred billion suns each larger than our sun.' After an interval President Roosevelt would grin and say: 'Now I think we are small enough. Let's go.'

ANONYMOUS

Hymn: Thou, Whose Almighty Word

Thou, whose almighty word
Chaos and darkness heard,
    And took their flight;
Hear us, we humbly pray,
And where the Gospel-day
Sheds not its glorious ray,
    Let there be light!

Thou, who didst come to bring
On thy redeeming wing
    Healing and sight,
Health to the sick in mind,
Sight to the inly blind,
O now to all mankind
    Let there be light!

Spirit of truth and love,
Life-giving, holy Dove,
    Speed forth thy flight;
Move on the water's face,
Bearing the lamp of grace,
And in earth's darkest place
    Let there be light!

Holy and blessèd Three,
Glorious Trinity,
   Wisdom, Love, Might;
Boundless as ocean's tide
Rolling in fullest pride,
Through the earth far and wide
   Let there be light!

J. MARRIOTT 1780–1825

4

LET THE WATERS BE GATHERED

O Lord Jesus Christ, who on the sea didst teach thy disciples many heavenly things, we pray thee to show the voice of thy truth and the power of thy presence to thy Church upon the deep, and be thou the guide and guardian of all that sail the seas; who livest and reignest with the Father and the Holy Ghost, one God, world without end.

ANONYMOUS

Where wast thou when I laid the foundations of the earth? declare, if thou hast understanding. Who hath laid the measures thereof, if thou knowest? or who hath stretched the line upon it? Whereupon are the foundations thereof fastened? or who laid the corner stone thereof; when the morning stars sang together, and all the sons of God shouted for joy? Or who shut up the sea with doors, when it brake forth, as if it had issued out of the womb?

Who hath divided a watercourse for the overflowing of waters, or a way for the lightning of thunder; to cause it to rain on the earth, where no man is; on the wilderness, wherein there is no man; to satisfy the desolate and waste ground; and to cause the bud of the tender herb to spring forth? Hath the rain a father? or who hath begotten the drops of dew? Out of whose womb came the ice? and the hoary frost of heaven, who hath gendered it? The waters are hid as with a stone, and the face of the deep is frozen.

JOB 38: 4–8, 25–30

And he showed me a pure river of water of life, clear as crystal, proceeding out of the throne of God and of the Lamb. In the midst of the street of it, and on either side of the river, was there the tree of life, which bare twelve manner of fruits, and yielded her fruit every month: and the leaves of the tree were for the healing of the nations.

REVELATION 22: 1–2

1 *And God Created the Great Whales*

And God created the great whales, and each
Soul living, each that crept, which plenteously
The waters generated by their kinds,
And every bird of wing after his kind;
And saw that it was good, and blessed them, saying,
Be fruitful, multiply, and in the seas
And lakes and running streams the waters fill;
And let the fowl be multiplied on the earth.
Forthwith the sounds and seas, each creek and bay
With fry innumerable swarm, and shoals
Of fish that with their fins and shining scales
Glide under the green wave, in schools that oft
Bank the mid sea: part single or with mate
Graze the sea weed their pasture, and through groves
Of coral stray, or sporting with quick glance
Show to the sun their waved coats dropped with gold,
Or in their pearly shells at ease, attend
Moist nutriment, or under rocks their food
In jointed armour watch: on smooth the seal,
And bended dolphins play; part huge of bulk
Wallowing unwieldy, enormous in their gait
Tempest the ocean: there leviathan
Hugest of living creatures, on the deep
Stretched like a promontory sleeps or swims
And seems a moving land, and at his gills
Draws in, and at his trunk spouts out a sea.

JOHN MILTON 1608–1674 *Paradise Lost*

2 *The Whale's Domain*

I can utter a true song about myself,
Tell of my travels, how in days of toil
I have suffered many hardships, endured many sorrows,
And made trial of my troublesome home upon the heaving
     waves.
The hard night watch at the ship's prow was often my task,
Oppressed by cold, my feet were fettered with frost in icy
     bonds;
While my sorrows seethed and simmered hot round my
     heart,
And hunger tore my body . . .
Sometimes the song of a wild swan was my pleasure;
Or the cries of gannets and curlews were for me the laughter
     of men,
And the screams of the gulls replaced mead in the hall.
Storms beat about the rocky cliffs;
The icy-feathered tern replied, the dewy-beaked eagle
     shrieked.
There was no comforter for my desolate spirit . . .
Yet my heart is again restless in my breast,
My mind is roaming to the tossing sea and the whale's
     domain.
My spirit travels widely over the face of the earth,
Returning to me eager and unsatisfied,
Resistlessly urging my heart towards the whale-way
And the stretch of seas.

                ANONYMOUS (Anglo-Saxon) 'The Seafarer'

3 *By the Sea*

Why does the sea moan evermore?
  Shut out from heaven it makes its moan,
It frets against the boundary shore:
  All earth's full rivers cannot fill
  The sea, that drinking thirsteth still.

Sheer miracles of loveliness
  Lie hid in its unlooked-on bed:
Anemones, salt, passionless,
  Blow flower-like – just enough alive
  To blow and multiply and thrive.

Shells quaint with curve or spot or spike,
  Encrusted live things argus-eyed,
All fair alike yet all unlike,
  Are born without a pang, and die
  Without a pang, and so pass by.

CHRISTINA ROSSETTI 1830–1894

4 *Consider the Sea's Listless Chime*

Consider the sea's listless chime:
  Time's self it is, made audible, –
  The murmur of the earth's own shell.
Secret continuance sublime
  Is the sea's end: our sight may pass
  No furlong further. Since time was,
This sound hath told the lapse of time.

No quiet, which is death's, – it hath
  The mournfulness of ancient life,
  Enduring always at dull strife.
As the world's heart of rest and wrath,

Its painful pulse is in the sands.
Last utterly, the whole sky stands,
Grey and not known, along its path . . .

Gather a shell from the strown beach
   And listen at its lips: they sigh
   The same desire and mystery,
The echo of the whole sea's speech.
   And all mankind is thus at heart
   Not anything but what thou art:
And Earth, Sea, Man, are all in each.

DANTE GABRIEL ROSSETTI 1828–1882 'The Sea's Limits'

5 *The Vast of the Lord*

And the sea lends large, as the marsh: lo, out of his plenty
     the sea
  Pours fast: full soon the time of the flood-tide must be:
   Look how the grace of the sea doth go
  About and about through the intricate channels that flow
    Here and there,
     Everywhere,
Till his waters have flooded the uttermost creeks and the
    low-lying lanes,
   And the marsh is meshed with a million veins,
  That like as with rosy and silvery essences flow
   In the rose-and-silver evening glow.
    Farewell, my lord Sun!
  The creeks overflow: a thousand rivulets run
  'Twixt the roots of the sod; the blades of the marsh-grass
    stir;
Passeth a hurrying sound of wings that westward whirr;
Passeth, and all is still; and the currents cease to run;
   And the sea and the marsh are one.

How still the plains of the waters be!
The tide is in his ecstasy.
The tide is at his highest height:
  And it is night.

And now from the Vast of the Lord will the waters of
    sleep
  Roll in on the souls of men.
But who will reveal to our waking ken
The forms that swim and the shapes that creep
  Under the waters of sleep?
And I would I could know what swimmeth below when
    the tide comes in
On the length and the breadth of the marvellous marshes
    of Glynn.

SIDNEY LANIER 1842–1881 'The Marshes of Glynn'

6 *The Sea is Calm To-night*

The sea is calm to-night,
The tide is full, the moon lies fair
Upon the Straits; – on the French coast the light
Gleams and is gone; the cliffs of England stand,
Glimmering and vast, out in the tranquil bay,
Come to the window, sweet is the night air!
Only, from the long line of spray
Where the ebb meets the moon-blanched sand,
Listen! you hear the grating roar
Of pebbles which the waves suck back, and fling,
At their return, up the high strand,
Begin, and cease, and then again begin,
With tremulous cadence slow, and bring
The eternal note of sadness in.

MATTHEW ARNOLD 1822–1888 'Dover Beach'

7 *The Moving Sea*

Is it not because it is always moving, and because one is not
moving with it that the sea means so much more to one
than any possible inland scenery? A tree, a meadow, though
it grows and changes, grows and changes imperceptibly; I
cannot see it in motion; it seems to be always there, irritat-
ingly immobile. But the sea is always moving past me; it is
like a friend who comes and goes and is faithful; its motion
is all I have to give me some sense of permanency in a world
where all things grow old and pass away, except the sea.
Byron was right, though he spoke pompously: 'Time writes
no wrinkle on thine azure brow'. Every part of the earth's
body is growing old, and shows the signs and scars of age;
only the sea is without that symptom of mortality, and
remains a witness to the original youth of creation.

ARTHUR SYMONS 1865–1945 *Cities and Sea-Coasts and Islands*

8 *Perfect Freedom*

They had tacked, and they were sailing swiftly, buoyantly
on long rocking waves which handed them on from one to
another with an extraordinary lilt and exhilaration beside the
reef. On the left a row of rocks showed brown through the
water which thinned and became greener and on one, a
higher rock, a wave incessantly broke and spurted a little
column of drops which fell down in a shower. One could
hear the slap of the water and the patter of falling drops and
a kind of hushing and hissing sound from the waves rolling
and gambolling and slapping the rocks as if they were wild
creatures who were perfectly free and tossed and tumbled
and sported like this for ever.

VIRGINIA WOOLF 1882–1941 *To the Lighthouse*

9 *The Flocks of the Storm*

It was against a seaport fortress, profoundly walled, that some remembered winter storms lately turned their great artillery. It was a time of resounding nights; the sky was so clamorous and so close, up in the towers of the stronghold, that one seemed to be indeed admitted to the perturbed counsels of the winds. The gale came with an indescribable haste, hooting as it flew; it seemed to break itself upon the heights, yet passed unbroken out to sea; in the voice of the sea there were pauses, but none in that of the urgent gale with its hoo-hoo-hoo all night, that clamoured down the calling of the waves. That lack of pauses was the strangest thing in the tempest, because the increase of sound seemed to imply a lull before. The lull was never perceptible, but the lift was always an alarm. The onslaught was instant, where would it stop? What was the secret extreme to which this hurry and force were tending? You asked less what thing was driving the flocks of the storm than what was calling them. And there were moments when the end seemed about to be attained.

ALICE MEYNELL 1849–1922 *From the Sea Wall*

10 *The Tide Rises, the Tide Falls*

The tide rises, the tide falls,
The twilight darkens, the curlew calls;
Along the sea-sands damp and brown
The traveller hastens toward the town,
    And the tide rises, the tide falls.

Darkness settles on roofs and walls,
But the sea, the sea in the darkness calls;

The little waves, with their soft, white hands,
Efface the footprints in the sands,
   And the tide rises, the tide falls.

The morning breaks; the steeds in their stalls
Stamp and neigh, as the hostler calls;
The day returns, but nevermore
Returns the traveller to the shore,
   And the tide rises, the tide falls.

HENRY WADSWORTH LONGFELLOW 1807–1882

11 *What Sweet Mystery*

There is one knows not what sweet mystery about this sea,
whose gently awful stirrings seem to speak of some hidden
soul beneath; like those fabled undulations of the Ephesian
sod over the buried evangelist, St. John. And meet it is, that
over these sea-pastures, wide-rolling, watery prairies and
Potters' Fields of all four continents, the waves should rise
and fall, and ebb and flow unceasingly; for here, millions of
mixed shades and shadows, drowned dreams, somnambu-
lisms, reveries; all that we call lives and souls, lie dreaming,
dreaming, still; tossed like slumberers in their beds; the ever-
rolling waves but made so by their restlessness.

To any meditative Magian rover, this serene Pacific once
beheld, must ever after be the sea of his adoption. It rolls
the midmost waters of the world, the Indian Ocean and
Atlantic being but its arms. The same waves wash the moles
of the new-built Californian towns, but yesterday planted
by the recentest race of men, and lave the faded but still
gorgeous skirts of Asiatic lands, older than Abraham; while
all between float milky-ways of coral isles, and low-lying,
endless, unknown Archipelagoes and impenetrable Japans.

Thus this mysterious, divine Pacific zones the world's whole bulk about; makes all coasts one bay to it; seems the tide-beating heart of earth. Lifted by those eternal swells, you needs must own the seductive god, bowing your head to Pan.

HERMAN MELVILLE 1819–1891 *Moby Dick*

12 *The Greatest Thing God Made*

'And what is the sea?' asked Will.

'The sea!' cried the miller. 'Lord help us all, it is the greatest thing God made! That is where all the water in the world runs down into a great salt lake. There it lies, as flat as my hand and as innocent-like as a child; but they do say when the wind blows it gets up into water-mountains bigger than any of ours, and swallows down great ships bigger than our mill, and makes such a roaring that you can hear it miles away upon the land. There are great fish in it five times bigger than a bull, and one old serpent as long as our river and as old as all the world, with whiskers like a man, and a crown of silver on her head.'

ROBERT LOUIS STEVENSON 1850–1894 *Will o' the Mill*

13 *A Kind and Beautiful Woman*

In the dark the old man could feel the morning coming and as he rowed he heard the trembling sound as flying fish left the water and the hissing that their stiff set wings made as they soared away in the darkness. He was very fond of flying fish as they were his principal friends on the ocean. He was sorry for the birds, especially the small delicate dark terns

that were always flying and looking and almost never finding, and he thought, 'The birds have a harder life than we
do except for the robber birds and the heavy strong ones.
Why did they make birds so delicate and fine as those sea
swallows when the ocean can be so cruel? She is kind and
very beautiful. But she can be so cruel and it comes so
suddenly and such birds that fly, dipping and hunting, with
their small sad voices are made too delicately for the sea.'

He always thought of the sea as *la mar* which is what
people call her in Spanish when they love her. Sometimes
those who love her say bad things of her but they are always
said as though she were a woman. Some of the younger
fishermen, those who used buoys as floats for their lines and
had motor-boats, bought when the shark livers had brought
much money, spoke of her as *el mar* which is masculine.
They spoke of her as a contestant or a place or even an
enemy. But the old man always thought of her as feminine
and as something that gave or withheld great favours, and
if she did wild or wicked things it was because she could
not help them. The moon affects her as it does a woman,
he thought.

ERNEST HEMINGWAY 1898–1961 *The Old Man and the Sea*

14 *The Sea's Glamour*

'I have known its fascination since: I have seen the mysterious
shores, the still water, the lands of brown nations, where a
stealthy Nemesis lies in wait, pursues, overtakes so many of
the conquering race, who are proud of their wisdom, of
their knowledge, of their strength. But for me all the East
is contained in that vision of my youth. It is all in that
moment when I opened my young eyes on it. I came upon
it from a tussle with the sea – and I was young – and I saw
it looking at me. And this is all that is left of it! Only a

moment; a moment of strength, of romance, of glamour –
of youth! . . . A flick of sunshine upon a strange shore, the
time to remember, the time for a sigh, and – good-bye! –
Night – Goodbye . . . !'

He drank.

'Ah! The good old time – the good old time. Youth and
the sea. Glamour and the sea! The good, strong sea, the salt,
bitter sea, that could whisper to you and roar at you and
knock your breath out of you.'

He drank again.

'By all that's wonderful, it is the sea, I believe, the sea
itself – or is it youth alone? Who can tell? But you here –
you all had something out of life: money, love – whatever
one gets on shore – and, tell me, wasn't that the best time,
that time when we were young at sea; young and had
nothing, on the sea that gives nothing, except hard knocks
– and sometimes a chance to feel your strength – that only
– what you all regret?'

JOSEPH CONRAD 1857–1924 *Youth*

15 *Clear and Cool*

Clear and cool, clear and cool,
By laughing shallow, and dreaming pool;
Cool and clear, cool and clear,
By shining shingle, and foaming wear;
Under the crag where the ouzel sings,
And the ivied wall where the churchbell rings,
Undefiled, for the undefiled;
Play by me, bathe in me, mother and child.

Dank and foul, dank and foul,
By the smoky town in its murky cowl;
Foul and dank, foul and dank,

By wharf and sewer and slimy bank;
Darker and darker the farther I go,
Baser and baser the richer I grow;
　　Who dare sport with the sin-defiled?
　Shrink from me, turn from me, mother and child.

　　Strong and free, strong and free,
　The floodgates are open, away to the sea,
　　Free and strong, free and strong,
　Cleansing my streams as I hurry along,
To the golden sands, and the leaping bar,
And the taintless tide that awaits me afar.
As I lose myself in the infinite main,
Like a soul that has sinned and is pardoned again.
　　Undefiled, for the undefiled;
　Play by me, bathe in me, mother and child.

　　　　CHARLES KINGSLEY 1819–1875 *The Water Babies*

16 *The Water Flows*

The water flows
Peacefully along . . .
Under the trees
Like a song
Unsung

Peacefully the water flows
Under the trees,
Brown water deep and cool,
Like beautiful words
That no one has said
For the lips that might have spoken them
Are dead,
But the words are there still
In the stream,

Carried along
With the silent song . . .

Gentle winding stream
Under the trees,
You are like a dream
That might have been dreamt
But the dreamer awoke
Too soon . . .

The dream is here
In the stream,
Carried along
With the song
And the words
That are too lovely to be said.

The stream ripples and murmurs,
It talks as it flows,
But it is not the stream that I hear,
It is the deep dream and the song and the rhythm of
          beautiful words.
They are there
Under the trees
Flowing along . . .
O song,
O words,
O dream,
You do not only *seem*,
You are there in the deep reality of final peace.

AGATHA CHRISTIE 1890–1976

17 *Under the Cooling Shadow*

Under the cooling shadow of a stately elm
Close sat I by a goodly river's side,
Where gliding streams the rocks did overwhelm,
A lonely place, with pleasures dignified.
I once that loved the shady woods so well,
Now thought the rivers did the trees excel,
And if the sun would ever shine, there would I dwell.

While on the stealing stream I fixed mine eye,
Which to the longed-for ocean held its course,
I marked, nor crooks, nor rubs that there did lie
Could hinder ought, but still augment its force.
'O happy flood,' quoth I, 'that holds thy race
Till thou arrive at thy beloved place,
Nor is it rocks or shoals that can obstruct thy pace;

Nor is't enough, that thou alone mayst slide,
But hundred brooks in thy clear waves do meet,
So hand in hand along with thee they glide
To Thetis' house, where all embrace and greet.
Thou emblem true of what I count the best,
O could I lead my rivulets to rest,
So may we press to that vast mansion, ever blest.'

Ye fish, which in this liquid region 'bide,
That for each season have your habitation,
Now salt, now fresh where you think best to glide
To unknown coasts to give a visitation,
In lakes and ponds you leave your numerous fry;
So nature taught, and yet you know not why,
You wat'ry folk that know not your felicity.

ANNE BRADSTREET 1612–1672 'Contemplations'

18 *A Babbling Procession*

He thought his happiness was complete when, as he meandered aimlessly along, suddenly he stood by the edge of a full-fed river. Never in his life had he seen a river before – this sleek, sinuous, full-bodied animal, chasing and chuckling, gripping things with a gurgle and leaving them with a laugh, to fling itself on fresh playmates that shook themselves free, and were caught and held again. All was a-shake and a-shiver – glints and gleams and sparkles, rustle and swirl, chatter and bubble. The Mole was bewitched, entranced, fascinated. By the side of the river he trotted as one trots, when very small, by the side of a man who holds one spellbound by exciting stories; and when, tired at last, he sat on the bank, while the river still chattered on to him, a babbling procession of the best stories in the world, sent from the heart of the earth to be told at last to the insatiable sea.

KENNETH GRAHAME 1859–1932 *The Wind in the Willows*

19 *I Love Rain*

At all times I love rain, the early momentous thunderdrops, the perpendicular cataract shining, or at night the little showers, the spongy mists, the tempestuous mountain rain. I like to see it possessing the whole earth at evening, smothering civilization, taking away from me myself everything except the power to walk under the dark trees and to enjoy as humbly as the hissing grass, while some twinkling house-light or song sung by a lonely man gives a foil to the immense dark force. I like to see the rain making the streets, the railway station, a pure desert, whether bright with lamps or not. It foams off the roofs and trees and bubbles into the water-butts. It gives the grey rivers a demonic majesty. It scours the roads, sets the flints moving, and exposes the glossy chalk in the tracks through the woods. It does work that will last as long as the earth. It is about eternal business. In its noise and myriad aspect I feel the mortal beauty of immortal things. And then after many days the rain ceases at midnight with the wind, and in the silence of dawn and frost the last rose of the world is dropping her petals down to the glistering whiteness, and there they rest blood-red on the winter's desolate coast.

EDWARD THOMAS 1878–1917 *The South Country*

20 *Delightful it is to Stand*

Delightful it is to stand on the peak of a rock, in the bosom of the isle, gazing on the face of the sea.

I hear the heaving waves chanting a tune to God in heaven; I see their glittering surf.

I see the golden beaches, their sands sparkling; I hear the joyous shrieks of the swooping gulls.

I hear the waves breaking, crashing on rocks, like thunder in heaven. I see the mighty whales.

I watch the ebb and flow of the ocean tide; it holds my secret, my mournful flight from Eire.

Contrition fills my heart as I hear the sea; it chants my sins, sins too numerous to confess.

Let me bless almighty God, whose power extends over sea and land, whose angels watch over all.

Let me study sacred books to calm my soul; I pray for peace, kneeling at heaven's gates.

Let me do my daily work, gathering seaweed, catching fish, giving food to the poor.

Let me say my daily prayers, sometimes chanting, sometimes quiet, always thanking God.

Delightful it is to live on a peaceful isle, in a quiet cell, serving the King of kings.

COLUMBA *d.* 597 attributed

Hymn: Jesu, Lover of my Soul

Jesu, lover of my soul,
Let me to thy bosom fly,
While the gathering waters roll,
While the tempest still is high:
Hide me, O my Saviour, hide,
Till the storm of life is past;
Safe into the haven guide,
O receive my soul at last.

Other refuge have I none;
Hangs my helpless soul on thee;
Leave, ah, leave me not alone,
Still support and comfort me.
All my trust on thee is stayed,
All my help from thee I bring;
Cover my defenceless head
With the shadow of thy wing.

Plenteous grace with thee is found,
Grace to cleanse from every sin;
Let the healing streams abound;
Make and keep me pure within:
Thou of life the fountain art;
Freely let me take of thee;
Spring thou up within my heart,
Rise to all eternity.

CHARLES WESLEY 1707–1788

5

LET DRY LAND APPEAR

Eternal and glorious Lord God, since thy glory and honour is the great end of all thy works, we desire that it may be the beginning and end of all our prayers. Let thy great name be glorious and sanctified throughout the earth. Let the knowledge of thee fill all the earth as the waters cover the sea. Let all thy works praise thee. May we have high and honourable thoughts concerning thee, in some measure suitable to thy glory, majesty, goodness, wisdom and bounty. Through Jesus Christ our Lord.

MATTHEW HALE 1609–1676 adapted

And the Lord spake unto Moses in mount Sinai, saying, Speak unto the children of Israel, and say unto them, When ye come into the land which I give you, then shall the land keep a sabbath unto the Lord. Six years thou shalt sow thy field, and six years thou shalt prune thy vineyard, and gather in the fruit thereof; but in the seventh year shall be a sabbath of rest unto the land, a sabbath for the Lord: thou shalt neither sow thy field, nor prune thy vineyard. That which groweth of its own accord of thy harvest thou shalt not reap, neither gather the grapes of thy vine undressed: for it is a year of rest unto the land.

LEVITICUS 25: 1–5

Behold, a sower went forth to sow; and when he sowed, some seeds fell by the way side, and the fowls came and devoured them up: some fell upon stony places, where they had not much earth: and forthwith they sprung up, because they had no deepness of earth: and when the sun was up, they were scorched; and because they had no root, they withered away. And some fell among thorns; and the thorns sprung up, and choked them: but other fell into good ground, and brought forth fruit, some an hundredfold, some sixtyfold, some thirtyfold.

MATTHEW 13: 3b–8

1 *Turn Out of the Way*

But turn out of the way a little, good Scholar, towards yonder high honeysuckle hedge; there we'll sit and sing whilst this shower falls so gently upon the teeming earth, and gives yet a sweeter smell to the lovely flowers that adorn these verdant meadows.

Look, under that broad beech-tree I sat down, when I was last this way a-fishing, and the birds in the adjoining grove seemed to have a friendly contention with an echo, whose dead voice seemed to live in a hollow tree, near to the brow of that primrose hill; there I sat viewing the silver streams glide silently towards their centre, the tempestuous sea; yet sometimes opposed by rugged roots, and pebble-stones, which broke their waves, and turned them into foam: and sometimes I beguiled time by viewing the harmless lambs, some leaping securely in the cool shade, whilst others sported themselves in the cheerful sun; and saw others craving comfort from the swollen udders of their bleating dams. As I thus sat these and other sights had so fully possessed my soul with content that I thought as the poet has happily expressed it,

'I was for that time lifted above earth,
And possessed joys not promised in my birth.'

IZAAK WALTON 1593–1683 *The Compleat Angler*

2 *A Sacred Veneration*

I had plenty of leisure, but it was the leisure of solitude, for my Sundays were demanded to be spent in the fields at horse or cow tending. My whole summer was one day's employment as it were. In the fields I grew so much into the quiet love of nature's preserves that I was never easy but

when I was in the fields passing my sabbaths and leisure
with the shepherds and herd boys, as fancies prompted –
sometimes playing at marbles on the smooth-beaten sheep
tracks or leapfrog among the thymy molehills; or running
into the woods to hunt strawberries; or stealing peas in
churchtime (when the owners were safe), to boil at the gip-
sies' fire, who went half-shares at our stolen luxury. We
heard the bells chime, but the fields was our church, and we
seemed to feel a religious piety in our haunts on the sabbath
– while some old shepherd sat on a molehill, reading aloud
some favourite chapter from an old fragment of a Bible,
which he carried in his pocket for the day. A family relic –
which possessed on its covers and title pages in rude scrawls
genealogies of the third and fourth generations; when aunts,
mothers and grandmothers died; when cousins etc. were
married and brothers and sisters born. Occupying all the
blank leaves in the book and title pages, which leaves were
preserved with a sacred veneration though half the contents
had been suffered to drop out and be lost.

JOHN CLARE 1793–1864 *Autobiography*

3 *The English Garden*

The plants and trees which grow in a garden, prefer, like
most others, the best soil that is to be found; and the best
is, good fat loam at the top, with a bottom that suffers the
wet gently to escape. But we must take that which we
happen to have, avoiding, if we possibly can, a stiff clay or
gravel, not only as a top-soil, but as a bottom-soil also,
unless at a very great distance. Oak-trees love clay, and the
finest of that sort of timber grows, on such land; but no
trees that grow in a garden love clay, and they are still less
fond of gravel, which always burns in summer time, and
which sucks up the manure, and carries it away out of the

reach of the roots of the plants. Chalk, if it be too near, to the top, is not good; but it is better than clay or gravel; and by the means of trenching, of which I shall presently speak, chalky soil may make a very good garden; for chalk never burns in summer, and is never wet in winter; that is to say, it never causes stagnant water. It absorbs it, and retains it, until drawn upwards by the summer sun. And hence it is that the chalky downs are fresh and green, while even the meadows in the valleys are burned up so as to be perfectly brown. No tree rejects chalk; chalk is not apt to produce canker in trees; and, upon the whole, it is not a bad soil even for a garden, while, if it have a tolerable depth of earth on the top of it, it is, taking all things together, the pasturage, the sound roads, the easy cultivation in all weathers, the healthiness which it invariably gives to cattle of all sorts, the very best land in the world for a farm; and I, who have perhaps seen as many farms and homesteads as any man in England, and in as many different situations, never saw such fine, such beautiful, such generally productive, such neat and really rich farms, as in countries consisting entirely of chalk, excepting the mere bottoms of the valleys along which run the brooks and the rivers, and here, too, are the finest of all the watered meadows that I ever saw.

WILLIAM COBBETT 1763–1835 *The English Gardener*

4 *Gardens of the Desert*

These are the gardens of the Desert, these
The unshorn fields, boundless and beautiful,
For which the speech of England has no name –
The Prairies. I behold them for the first,
And my heart swells, while the dilated sight
Takes in the encircling vastness. Lo! they stretch,
In airy undulations, far away,

As if the ocean, in his gentlest swell,
Stood still, with all his rounded billows fixed,
And motionless forever. – Motionless? –
No – they are all unchained again. The clouds
Sweep over with their shadows, and, beneath,
The surface rolls and fluctuates to the eye;
Dark hollows seem to glide along and chase
The sunny ridges. Breezes of the South!
Who toss the golden and the flame-like flowers,
And pass the prairie-hawk that, poised on high,
Flaps his broad wings, yet moves not – ye have played
Among the palms of Mexico and vines
Of Texas, and have crisped the limpid brooks
That from the fountains of Sonora glide
Into the calm Pacific – have ye fanned
A nobler or a lovelier scene than this?
Man hath no power in all this glorious work:
The hand that built the firmament hath heaved
And smoothed these verdant swells, and sown their slopes
With herbage, planted them with island groves,
And hedged them round with forests. Fitting floor
For this magnificent temple of the sky –
With flowers whose glory and whose multitude
Rival the constellations! The great heavens
Seem to stoop down upon the scene in love, –
A nearer vault, and of a tenderer blue,
Than that which bends above our eastern hills.

WILLIAM CULLEN BRYANT 1794–1878 'The Prairies'

5 *A Midsummer Noon in the Australian Forest*

Not a sound disturbs the air,
There is quiet everywhere;
Over plains and over woods
What a mighty stillness broods!

All the birds and insects keep
Where the coolest shadows sleep;
Even the busy ants are found
Resting in their pebbled mound;
Even the locust clingeth now
Silent to the barky bough:
Over hills and over plains
Quiet, vast and slumbrous, reigns.

Only there's a drowsy humming
From yon warm lagoon slow coming:
'Tis the dragon-hornet – see!
All bedaubed resplendently,
Yellow on a tawny ground –
Each rich spot nor square nor round,
Rudely heart-shaped, as it were
The blurred and hasty impress there
Of a vermeil-crusted seal,
Dusted o'er with golden meal.
Only there's a droning where
Yon bright beetle shines in air,
Tracks it in its gleaming flight,
With a slanting beam of light,
Rising in the sunshine higher,
Till its shards flame out like fire.

Every other thing is still,
Save the ever-wakeful rill,
Whose cool murmur only throws
Cooler comfort round repose;

Or some ripple in the sea
Of leafy boughs, where, lazily,
Tired summer, in her bower
Turning with the noontide hour,
Heaves a slumbrous breath ere she
Once more slumbers peacefully.

O, 'tis easeful here to lie
Hidden from noon's scorching eye,
In this grassy cool recess
Musing thus of quietness.

CHARLES HARPUR 1813–1868

6 *Majesty and Grace*

Rarely are Mountains seen in such combined majesty and
grace as here. The rocks are of that sort called Primitive by
the mineralogists, which always arrange themselves in
masses of a rugged, gigantic character; which ruggedness,
however, is here tempered by a singular airiness of form,
and softness of environment: in a climate favourable to veg-
etation, the gray cliff, itself covered with lichens, shoots up
through a garment of foliage or verdure; and white, bright
cottages, tree-shaded, cluster round the everlasting granite.
In fine vicissitude, Beauty alternates with Grandeur: you
ride through stony hollows, along strait passes, traversed by
torrents, overhung by high walls of rock; now winding amid
broken shaggy chasms, and huge fragments; now suddenly
emerging into some emerald valley, where the streamlet
collects itself into a Lake, and man has again found a fair
dwelling, and it seems as if Peace had established herself in
the bosom of Strength . . .
Now the Valley closes in abruptly, intersected by a huge
mountain mass, the stony waterworn ascent of which is not

to be accomplished on horseback. Arrived aloft, he finds himself again lifted into the evening sunset light; and cannot but pause, and gaze round him, some moments there. An upland irregular expanse of wold, where valleys in complex branchings are suddenly or slowly arranging their descent towards every quarter of the sky. The mountain-ranges are beneath your feet, and folded together: only the loftier summits look down here and there as on a second plain; lakes also lie clear and earnest in their solitude. No trace of man now visible; unless indeed it were he who fashioned that little visible link of Highway, here, as would seem, scaling the inaccessible, to unite Province with Province. But sunwards, to you! how it towers sheer up, a world of Mountains, the diadem and centre of the mountain region! A hundred and a hundred savage peaks, in the last light of Day; all glowing, of gold and amethyst, like giant spirits of the wilderness; there in their silence, in their solitude, even as on the night when Noah's Deluge first dried!

THOMAS CARLYLE 1795–1881 *Sartor Resartus*

7 *The Lady of the Hills*

The Lady of the Hills with crimes untold
Followed my feet with azure eyes of prey;
By glacier-brink she stood – by cataract-spray –
When mists were dire, or avalanche-echoes rolled.
At night she glimmered in the death-wind cold,
And if a footprint shone at break of day,
My flesh would quail, but straight my soul would say:
''Tis hers whose hand God's mightier hand doth hold.'
I trod her snow-bridge, for the moon was bright,
Her icicle-arch across the sheer crevasse,
When lo, she stood! – God made her let me pass,
Then felled the bridge! – Oh, there in sallow light,

There down the chasm, I saw her cruel, white,
And all my wondrous days as in a glass . . .

What power is this? what witchery wins my feet
To peaks so sheer they scorn the cloaking snow,
All silent as the emerald gulfs below,
Down whose ice-walls the wings of twilight beat?
What thrill of earth and heaven – most wild, most sweet –
What answering pulse that all the senses know,
Comes leaping from the ruddy eastern glow
Where, far away, the skies and mountains meet?
Mother, 'tis I reborn: I know thee well:
That throb I know and all it prophesies,
O Mother and Queen, beneath the olden spell
Of silence, gazing from thy hills and skies!
Dumb Mother, struggling with the years to tell
The secret at thy heart through helpless eyes.

THEODORE WATTS-DUNTON 1832–1914 'The Coming of Love'

8 Physical and Spiritual

Though I were stricken with blindness I would still go to
the mountains. I would lie on the turf of a quiet alp in the
morning, when the dew is drying, and the light breezes are
fragrant with flowers and moist earth. I would breathe long
breaths of pine-scented airs. I would hearken to the lazy
jangle of cowbells from distant pastures, the boom of glacier
torrents, and the solemn roll of avalanches. And, maybe, the
'Lordly Folk who dwell in the Hollow Hills' would take
pity upon me: I would hear their friendly chuckles in the
near-by stream, their elfin whispers in the grass, and their
murmured chorus in the pine-tops.

   Or I would ask to be led to some high hut and, lying on
its straw-filled bunks, listen to the deep voice of the night

wind, and in the early morning open the door and, going forth, meet the keen dawn-breath with its indefinable promise of delight.

Or possibly I would be content with the homeland hills, and sitting on a windy edge inhale deeply the salt tang of the sea, or spend a day on a soft couch of heather in some silent cwm or glen, and share the confidences of the small hill-stream on its journey to the sea.

A full appreciation of mountains is not to be experienced by merely looking; that is why men climb. On this earth the physical is an essential complement of the spiritual.

F. S. SMYTHE 1900–1949 *Climbs and Ski Runs*

9 *Soft Violence of Prayer*

Forced by soft violence of prayer,
The blithesome goddess soothes my care;
I feel the deity inspire,
And thus she models my desire.
Two hundred pounds, half-yearly paid,
Annuity securely made,
A farm some twenty miles from town,
Small, tight, salubrious, and my own:
Two maids, that never saw the town,
A serving man not quite a clown;
A boy to help to tread the mow,
And drive, while t'other holds the plough;
A chief, of temper formed to please,
Fit to converse, and keep the keys;
And better to preserve the peace,
Commissioned by the name of niece;
With understandings of a size
To think their master very wise.
May Heaven ('tis all I wish for) send
One genial room to treat a friend,

Where decent cupboard, little plate,
Display benevolence, not state.
And may my humble dwelling stand
Upon some chosen spot of land:
A pond before full to the brim,
Where cows may cool, and geese may swim;
Behind a green, like velvet neat,
Soft to the eye and to the feet;
Where odorous plants, in evening fair,
Breathe all around ambrosial air;
From Eurus, foe to kitchen ground,
Fenced by a slope with bushes crowned,
Fit dwelling for the feathered throng,
Who pay their quitrents with a song;
With opening views of hill and dale,
Which sense and fancy too regale,
Where the half-cirque, which vision bounds,
Like amphitheatre surrounds;
And woods, impervious to the breeze,
Thick phalanx of embodied trees,
From hills through plains in dusk array
Extended far, repel the day.

MATTHEW GREEN 1696–1737 'The Spleen'

10 *The Poplar Field*

The poplars are felled; farewell to the shade
And the whispering sound of the cool colonnade:
The winds play no longer and sing in the leaves,
Nor Ouse on his bosom their image receives.

Twelve years have elapsed since I first took a view
Of my favourite field, and the bank where they grew:
And now in the grass behold they are laid,
And the tree is my seat that once lent me a shade.

The blackbird has fled to another retreat
Where the hazels afford him a screen from the heat;
And the scene where his melody charmed me before
Resounds with his sweet-flowing ditty no more.

My fugitive years are all hasting away,
And I must ere long lie as lowly as they,
With a turf on my breast and a stone at my head,
Ere another such grove shall arise in its stead.

'Tis a sight to engage me, if anything can,
To muse on the perishing pleasures of man;
Short-lived as we are, our enjoyments, I see,
Have a still shorter date, and die sooner than we.

WILLIAM COWPER 1731–1800

11 *Old Wild Lost Religion*

'Let us go right into the wood out of the quarry,' said Leslie.
'I have not been since I was a little lad.'

'It is trespassing,' said Emily.

'We don't trespass,' he replied grandiloquently.

So we went along by the hurrying brook, which fell over
little cascades in its haste, never looking once at the primroses
that were glimmering all along its banks. We turned aside,
and climbed the hill through the woods. Velvety green sprigs
of dog-mercury were scattered on the red soil. We came to
the top of a slope, where the wood thinned. As I talked to
Emily I became dimly aware of a whiteness over the ground.
She exclaimed with surprise, and I found that I was walking,
in the first shades of twilight, over clumps of snowdrops.
The hazels were thin, and only here and there an oak tree
uprose. All the ground was white with snowdrops, like
drops of manna scattered over the red earth, on the grey-
green cluster of leaves. There was a deep little dell, sharp

sloping like a cup, and a white sprinkling of flowers all the way down, with white flowers showing pale among the first inpouring of shadow at the bottom. The earth was red and warm, pricked with the dark, succulent green of bluebell sheaths, and embroidered with grey-green clusters of spears, and many white flowerets. High above, above the light tracery of hazel, the weird oaks tangled in the sunset. Below, in the first shadows, drooped hosts of little white flowers, so silent and sad; it seemed like a holy communion of pure wild things, numberless, frail, and folded meekly in the evening light. Other flower companies are glad; stately barbaric hordes of blue-bells, merry-headed cowslip groups, even light, tossing wood anemones; but snowdrops are sad and mysterious. We have lost their meaning. They do not belong to us, who ravish them. The girls bent among them, touching them with their fingers, and symbolizing the yearning which I felt. Folded in the twilight, these conquered flowerets are sad like forlorn little friends of dryads.

'What do they mean, do you think?' said Lettie in a low voice, as her white fingers touched the flowers, and her black furs fell on them.

'There are not so many this year,' said Leslie.

'They remind me of mistletoe, which is never ours, though we wear it,' said Emily to me.

'What do you think they say – what do they make you think, Cyril?' Lettie repeated.

'I don't know. Emily says they belong to some old wild lost religion. They were the symbol of tears, perhaps, to some strange-hearted Druid folk before us.'

'More than tears,' said Lettie. 'More than tears, they are so still. Something out of an old religion, that we have lost. They make me feel afraid.'

'What should you have to fear?' asked Leslie.

'If I knew, I shouldn't fear,' she answered. 'Look at all the snowdrops,' – they hung in dim, strange flecks among the dusky leaves – 'look at them – closed up, retreating, powerless. They belong to some knowledge we have lost, that I have lost and that I need. I feel afraid. They seem like something in fate. Do you think, Cyril, we can lose things off the earth – like mastodons, and those old monstrosities – but things that matter – wisdom?'

'It is against my creed,' said I.

'I believe I have lost something,' said she.

D. H. LAWRENCE 1885–1930 The White Peacock

12 *Inward Hearing*

It was very early, and the wood was in a charmed stillness. The blackbird fell into a long meditation, and Amber shut her eyes, listening, not with the ear, but with the soul. Here, where the sounds of the world died away like a lapsing tide, she heard the sad rumour that life makes, stirring and murmuring in the silver hush of nonentity. She heard the moth-flicker of worlds slipping out into their age-long life, and their return – faint as the hum of a spent bee – to their everlastingly mysterious cause. Leaning against a wild pear tree, she was aware, by her inward hearing, of the tidal wave of sap that rose so full and strong that she could almost imagine it roaring like the sea. Then a tremor of wind shook the flowering tree-tops, and she awoke again to the senses, to the strangeness of these utterances of the leaves . . . She had the feeling, almost of greed, that such days bring – days with something glistening in them, a touch of the eternal. She felt like a child on the sea beach, loaded with shells veined with rainbow tints, pearly, fiery, and all with the sea in them – all remembering the deep water. Every petal, every leaf, seemed to be conning some memory of profundities whence it had come. Every curving flower seemed full of echoes too majestic for its fragility. She climbed to the buckthorn grove. There they stood, creating their own atmosphere, as do all groups of trees. They dwelt in green fire, for their leaves – thin as those of the beeches – were young and fresh. Their stems were of regal purple. Their creamy flowers, long-stalked, five-petalled, sweet, starred the bases of the leaf clusters. Near by were the spindles, gracious with shining leaves and mysterious fourfold flowers. At the top of the inclosure was an old hedge of white-beams, that had ceased to be a hedge and become trees. The upward, springing boughs, the soft and downy leaves, were drifted over by flowers, so that each tree seemed to stand amazed at its own whiteness, like a young bride in an ample veil. A breath of scented air came from the hill tops and stole among the branches. That which had form, and knew the mortality which is in form, trembled before that which passed, formless and immortal. It seemed content to linger here for a little while, before the momentary existence of this visible beauty slipped into nothingness; but it did not commit its whole self to any creature of matter, neither to dew-dark petal nor gold-eyed bird. It passed in the wood, as sunlight passes, or as the wind goes by, lifting the leaves with indifferent fingers, or like the rain, stroking the flowers in childlike carelessness. Because of it the place became no mere congregation of trees, but a thing fierce as interstellar space. Yet in the wood it never nested, never came homing to the spangled meadow. For it possesses itself for ever in a vitality withheld, immutable. It was this that drew Amber with breathless curiosity into the secret haunts of nature. It was this that struck her now into a kind of ecstasy, so that she neither saw nor heard the stranger who came down the hill and stood watching her beneath the blossom.

MARY WEBB 1881–1927 *The House in Dormer Forest*

13 *Larches*

Larches are most fitting small red hills
That rise like swollen ant-heaps likeably
And modest before big things like near Malvern
Or Cotswold's further early Italian
Blue arrangement; unassuming as the
Cowslips, celandines, buglewort and daisies
That trinket out the green swerves like a child's game.
O never so careless or lavish as here.
I thought, 'You beauty! I must rise soon one dawn time
And ride to see the first beam strike on you
Of gold or ruddy recognisance over
Crickley level or Bredon sloping down.
I must play tunes like Burns, or sing like David,
A saying-out of what the hill leaves unexpressed,
The tale or song that lives in it, and is sole,
A round red thing, green upright things of flame'.
It is May, and the conceited cuckoo toots and whoos his
    name.

IVOR GURNEY 1890–1937

14 *Let It Work*

The trees were the worst loss and damage, for at Sharkey's
bidding they had been cut down recklessly far and wide over
the Shire; and Sam grieved over this more than anything
else. For one thing, this hurt would take long to heal, and
only his great-grandchildren, he thought, would see the
Shire as it ought to be.

Then suddenly one day, for he had been too busy for
weeks to give a thought to his adventures, he remembered
the gift of Galadriel. He brought the box out and showed it

to the other Travellers (for so they were now called by everyone), and asked their advice.

'I wondered when you would think of it,' said Frodo. 'Open it!'

Inside it was filled with a grey dust, soft and fine, in the middle of which was a seed, like a small nut with a silver shale. 'What can I do with this?' said Sam.

'Throw it in the air on a breezy day and let it do its work!' said Pippin.

'On what?' said Sam.

'Choose one spot as a nursery, and see what happens to the plants there,' said Merry.

'But I'm sure the Lady would not like me to keep it all for my own garden, now so many folk have suffered,' said Sam.

'Use all the wits and knowledge you have of your own, Sam,' said Frodo, 'and then use the gift to help your work and better it. And use it sparingly. There is not much here, and I expect every grain has a value.'

So Sam planted saplings in all the places where specially beautiful or beloved trees had been destroyed, and he put a grain of the precious dust in the soil at the root of each. He went up and down the Shire in this labour; but if he paid special attention to Hobbiton and Bywater no one blamed him. And at the end he found that he still had a little of the dust left; so he went to the Three-Farthing Stone, which is as near the centre of the Shire as no matter, and cast it in the air with his blessing. The little silver nut he planted in the Party Field where the tree had once been; and he wondered what would come of it. All through the winter he remained as patient as he could, and tried to restrain himself from going round constantly to see if anything was happening.

Spring surpassed his wildest hopes. His trees began to sprout and grow, as if time was in a hurry and wished to make one year do for twenty. In the Party Field a beautiful young sapling leaped up: it had silver bark and long leaves

and burst into golden flowers in April. It was indeed a
mallorn, and it was the wonder of the neighbourhood. In
after years, as it grew in grace and beauty, it was known far
and wide and people would come long journeys to see it:
the only *mallorn* west of the Mountains and east of the Sea,
and one of the finest in the world.

J. R. R. TOLKIEN 1892–1973 *The Return of the King*

15 *Whereas I Live*

Whereas I live, a pleasant life,
   and free from cruel hands,
I would not leave the pleasant field
   for all the townish lands.
For since that Pride is placèd thus,
   and Vice set up so high,
And Cruelty doth rage so sore,
   and men live all awry,
Think'st you that God will long forbear
   his scourge and plague to send
To such as him do still despise,
   and never seek to mend?
Let them be sure he will revenge
   when they think least upon.
But look a stormy shower doth rise
   which will fall here anon.
Menaclas, best we now depart,
   my cottage us shall keep,
For there is room for thee and me,
   and also for our sheep;
Some chestnuts have I there in store
   with cheese and pleasant whey.
God sends me vitals for my need,
   and I sing Care away.

BARNABE GOOGE 1540–1594 'Egloga Tertia'

16 *Harmony Through Discord*

Trees refresh the commonplaces of life, shed a harmony
through the busy discord, and appeal to those first sources
of emotion, which are associated with the remembrance of
all that is young and innocent. They seem also to present us
with a portion of the tranquillity we think we are labouring
for, and the desire of which is felt as an earnest that we shall
realize it somewhere, either in this world or in the next.
Above all, they render us more cheerful for the performance
of present duties; and the smallest seed of this kind, dropped
into the heart of man, is worth more, and may terminate in
better fruits, than anybody but a great poet could tell us.

LEIGH HUNT 1784–1859 *The Town*

17 *Hail, Old Patrician Trees*

Hail, old *Patrician* trees, so great and good!
    Hail, ye *Plebeian* underwood!
    Where the poetique birds rejoice,
And for their quiet nests and plenteous food
    Pay with their grateful voice.

Hail, the poor Muses' richest manor seat!
    Ye country houses and retreat,
    Which all the happy Gods so love,
That for you oft they quit their bright and great
    Metropolis above.

Here Nature does a house for me erect,
    Nature, the wisest architect,
    Who those fond artists does despise
That can the fair and living trees neglect;
    Yet the dead timber prize.

Here let me, careless and unthoughtful lying,
Hear the soft winds, above me flying,
With all their wanton boughs dispute,
And the more tuneful birds to both replying,
Nor be myself, too mute.

ABRAHAM COWLEY 1618–1667 'Of Solitude'

18 *Nature's Plough*

When we behold a wide, turf-covered expanse, we should
remember that its smoothness, on which so much of its
beauty depends, is mainly due to all the inequalities having
been slowly levelled by worms. It is a marvellous reflection
that the whole of the superficial mould over any such expanse
has passed, and will again pass, every few years through the
bodies of worms. The plough is one of the most ancient and
most valuable of man's inventions; but long before he existed
the land was in fact regularly ploughed, and still continues
to be thus ploughed by earth-worms. It may be doubted
whether there are many other animals which have played so
important a part in the history of the world, as have these
lowly organized creatures.

CHARLES DARWIN 1809–1882
The Formation of Vegetable Mould through the Action of Worms

19 *The Ant Farmer*

Ants also cultivate plants for food. These are the leaf-cutting
ants of tropical America, which can defoliate large trees
overnight. The leaf fragments, up to 2 cm across, are
brought into special chambers in the nests: one observer
described how the ants marched in 'like Sunday-school chil-

dren carrying banners' . . . In the chambers the leaf fragments are chewed up and, with other vegetable debris and
ant excrement, a hot-bed is created upon which a special
fungus grows, in principle exactly like a modern mushroom
grower's beds. The worker ants actively tend these fungi,
weeding out any alien growths that may appear, and trans-
plant the fungi to new chambers as these are prepared. Something in the ants' saliva inhibits the growth of unwanted
fungi and may also promote the wanted fungus's growth.
This fungus, which forms the major food of these ants, is a
small subterranean species which has never been seen outside
the ants' nests, although this may well be simply because of
the problem of knowing where to look. Neither is it known
whether the fungus lives naturally in the soil and was orig-
inally deliberately brought in by the ants, or grew in their
nests by accident and was then cultivated.

ANTHONY HUXLEY *b.* 1920 *Plant and Planet*

20 *Of Composts*

Of composts shall the muse descend to sing,
Nor soil her heavenly plumes? The sacred muse
Nought sordid deems, but what is base; nought fair
Unless true virtue stamp it with her seal.
Then, planter, wouldst thou double thine estate,
Never, ah! never be ashamed to tread
Thy dung-heaps, where the refuse of thy mills,
With all the ashes all thy coppers yield,
With weeds, mould, dung, and stale, a compost
        form,
Of force to fertilize the poorest soil.
  But, planter, if thy lands lie far remote,
And of access are difficult; on these
Leave the cane's sapless foliage; and with pens
Wattled (like those the muse hath oft times seen,

When frolic fancy led her youthful steps
In green Dorchestria's plains), the whole enclose:
There well thy stock with provender supply;
The well-fed stock will soon that food repay.
  Some of the skilful teach, and some deny,
That yams improve the soil. In meagre lands,
'Tis known the yam will ne'er to bigness swell;
And from each mould the vegetable tribes,
However frugal, nutriment derive:
Yet may their sheltering vines, their drooping leaves,
Their roots dividing the tenacious glebe,
More than refund the sustenance they draw.
  Whether the fattening compost in each hole
'Tis best to throw, or on the surface spread,
Is undetermined: trials must decide.
Unless kind rains and fostering dews descend,
To melt the compost's fertilizing salts,
A stinted plant, deceitful of thy hopes,
Will from those beds slow spring where hot dung
        lies:
But, if 'tis scattered generously o'er all,
The cane will better bear the solar blaze;
Less rain demand; and, by repeated crops
Thy land improved, its gratitude will show.

JAMES GRAINGER *c.* 1721–1766 'The Sugar-Cane'

Hymn: Hills of the North, Rejoice

Hills of the north, rejoice;
    River and mountain-spring,
Hark to the advent voice;
    Valley and lowland, sing:
Though absent long, your Lord is nigh;
He judgement brings and victory.

Isles of the southern seas,
    Deep in your coral caves
Pent be each warring breeze,
    Lulled be your restless waves:
He comes to reign with boundless sway,
And makes your wastes his great highway.

Lands of the east, awake,
    Soon shall your sons be free;
The sleep of ages break,
    And rise to liberty.
On your far hills, long cold and grey,
Has dawned the everlasting day.

Shores of the utmost west,
    Ye that have waited long,
Unvisited, unblest,
    Break forth to swelling song;
High raise the note, that Jesus died,
Yet lives and reigns, the Crucified.

Shout, while ye journey home;
    Songs be in every mouth;
Lo, from the north we come,
    From east and west and south.
City of God, the bond are free,
We come to live and reign in thee!

C. E. OAKLEY 1832–1865

6

LET THE EARTH PUT FORTH PLANTS

Almighty and everlasting God, who hast given to us the fruits of the earth in their season, and hast crowned the year with thy goodness: Give us grateful hearts, that we may unfeignedly thank thee for all thy loving-kindness, and worthily magnify thy holy name; through Jesus Christ our Lord.

JOHN DOWDEN 1840–1910

Thou visitest the earth, and waterest it: thou greatly enrichest it with the river of God, which is full of water: thou preparest them corn, when thou hast so provided for it. Thou waterest the ridges thereof abundantly: thou settlest the furrows thereof: thou makest it soft with showers: thou blessest the springing thereof. Thou crownest the year with thy goodness; and thy paths drop fatness.

PSALM 65: 9–11

Therefore I say unto you, Take no thought for your life, what ye shall eat, or what ye shall drink; nor yet for your body, what ye shall put on. Is not the life more than meat, and the body than raiment?

Behold the fowls of the air: for they sow not, neither do they reap, nor gather into barns; yet your heavenly Father feedeth them. Are ye not much better than they? Which of you by taking thought can add one cubit unto his stature? And why take ye thought for raiment? Consider the lilies of the field, how they grow; they toil not, neither do they spin: and yet I say unto you, That even Solomon in all his glory was not arrayed like one of these. Wherefore, if God so clothe the grass of the field, which today is, and tomorrow is cast into the oven, shall he not much more clothe you, O ye of little faith?

Therefore take no thought, saying, What shall we eat? or, What shall we drink? or, Wherewithal shall we be clothed? (For after all these things do the Gentiles seek:) for your heavenly Father knoweth that ye have need of all these things. But seek ye first the kingdom of God, and his righteousness: and all these things shall be added unto you.

MATTHEW 6: 25–33

1 *When in April*

When in April the sweet showers fall
And pierce the drought of March to the root, and all
The veins are bathed in liquor of such power
As brings about the engendering of the flower,
When also Zephyrus with his sweet breath
Exhales an air in every grove and heath
Upon the tender shoots, and the young sun
His half-course in the sign of the *Ram* has run,
And the small fowl are making melody
That sleep away the night with open eye
(So nature pricks them and their heart engages)
Then people long to go on pilgrimages
And palmers long to seek the stranger strands
Of far-off saints, hallowed in sundry lands,
And specially, from every shire's end
In England, down to Canterbury they wend
To seek the holy blissful martyr, quick
To give his help to them when they were sick.

GEOFFREY CHAUCER *c.* 1343–1400
'The Prologue' from *The Canterbury Tales*

2 *Apparelled with Plants*

For if delight may provoke men's labour, what greater
delight is there than to behold the earth apparelled with
plants, as with a robe of embroidered work, set with Orient
pearls and garnished with great diversity of rare and costly
jewels? If this variety and perfection of colours may affect
the eye, it is such in herbs and flowers that no Apelles, no
Zeuxis, ever could by any art express the like: if odours or
if taste may work satisfaction they are both so sovereign in
plants and so comfortable that no confection of the

apothecaries can equal their excellent virtue. But these delights are in the outward senses; the principal delight is in the mind, singularly enriched with the knowledge of these visible things, setting forth to us the invisible wisdom and admirable workmanship of Almighty God.

JOHN GERARD 1545–1612 *Herbal*

3 *How Vainly Men Themselves Amaze*

How vainly men themselves amaze
To win the palm, the oak, or bays;
And their uncessant labours see
Crowned from some single herb or tree,
Whose short and narrow vergèd shade
Does prudently their toils upbraid;
While all flowers and all trees do close
To weave the garlands of repose . . .

What wond'rous life is this I lead!
Ripe apples drop about my head;
The luscious clusters of the vine
Upon my mouth do crush their wine;
The nectarine, and curious peach,
Into my hands themselves do reach;
Stumbling on melons, as I pass,
Insnared with flowers, I fall on grass.

Meanwhile the mind, from pleasure less,
Withdraws into its happiness:
The mind, that ocean where each kind
Does straight its own resemblance find;
Yet it creates, transcending these,
Far other worlds, and other seas,
Annihilating all that's made
To a green thought in a green shade.

ANDREW MARVELL 1621–1678 'The Garden'

4 *My Master hath a Garden*

My master hath a garden, full-filled with divers flowers,
Where thou may'st gather posies gay, all times and hours,
     Here nought is heard
     But paradise-bird,
     Harp, dulcimer and lute,
     With cymbal,
     And timbrel,
     And the gentle sounding flute.

Oh! Jesus, Lord, my heal and weal, my bliss complete,
Make thou my heart thy garden-plot, true, fair and neat,
     That I may hear
     This music clear,
     Harp, dulcimer and lute,
     With cymbal,
     And timbrel,
     And the gentle sounding flute.

ANONYMOUS (Medieval)

5 *The Parson's Garden*

Now both the reading, and the knowing of herbs, may be done at such times as they may be a help and a recreation to more divine studies, nature serving grace both in the comfort of diversion, and the benefit of application when need requires. As also, by way of illustration, our Saviour made plants and seeds to teach the people: for he was the true householder, who bringeth out of his treasure things new and old; the old things of philosophy, and the new of grace; and maketh the one serve the other. And I conceive, our Saviour did this for three reasons: first, that by familiar things he might make his doctrine slip the more easily into the hearts even of the meanest. Secondly, that labouring people (whom he chiefly considered) might have everywhere monuments of his doctrine, remembering in gardens, his mustard-seed, and lilies; in the field, his seed-corn, and tares; and so not be drowned altogether in the works of their vocation, but sometimes lift up their minds to better things, even in the midst of their pains. Thirdly, that he might set a copy for parsons.

In the knowledge of simples, wherein the manifold wisdom of God is wonderfully to be seen, one thing would be carefully observed; which is, to know what herbs may be used instead of drugs of the same nature, and to make the garden the shop: for home-bred medicines are both more easy for the parson's purse, and more familiar for all men's bodies. Accordingly for salves, his wife seeks not the city, but prefers her garden and fields, before all outlandish gums. And surely hyssop, valerian, mercury, adder's tongue, yerrow, melilot, and St. John's-wort made into a salve; and elder, camomile, mallows, comphrey and smallage made into a poultice, have done great and rare cures. In curing of any, the parson and his family use to promise prayers, for this is to cure like a parson, this raiseth the action from the shop, to the church.

GEORGE HERBERT 1593–1633 *The Country Parson*

6 *The Vicarage Garden*

The love of flowers is so universal, and the garden may be such a useful adjunct to the cottage, yet there is very great ignorance of the right principles of gardening, and the parson may be of great use to his poorer neighbours, not only by teaching, but still more by showing them better ways in his own garden. For the parsonage garden gate should be always open, and every parishioner welcomed; there need be no fear of any undue advantage being taken of the free permission to enter – the one difficulty will be to induce them to come in. And the parson may do much to brighten the gardens of his parish, and so to increase the interest in them by giving plants from his own garden. I have for many years been a cultivator of hardy plants, and have been able to gather together a large number of species; and I was long ago taught, and have always held, that it is impossible to get or keep a large collection except by constant liberality in giving.

HENRY ELLACOMBE 1822–1916 *In a Gloucestershire Garden*

7 *The Garden as a Library*

The world is a great library, and fruit trees are some of the books wherein we may read and see plainly the attributes of God, his power, wisdom, goodness etc., and be instructed and taught our duty towards him in many things, even from fruit trees: for as trees (in a metaphorical sense) are books, so likewise in the same sense they have a voice, and speak plainly to us and teach us many good lessons.

All creatures (as a holy man says) have a teaching voice. They read us divinity lectures of divine providence . . .

How much of the goodness and excellence of God do fruit trees show forth when they (in their seasons) flourish with leaves, blossoms and fruits; especially considered not only as they appear beautiful to the eye, but with all their inward beauties and perfections, their virtues and uses in the life of man, both in alimental and physical respects; but most of all as they are similitudes and bear the figure and resemblance of many high and great mysteries in the Word of God: the analogy and resemblance of what is of the highest esteem with God, his people, his jewels, his adopted sons, yea his natural Son, as we frequently find in Scripture?

Fruit trees discover many things of God, and many things of ourselves, and concerning our duty to God. We enquire of and discourse with fruit trees when we consider and meditate on them, when we search out their virtues and perfections which God hath put into them, when we pry into their natures and properties, that is speaking to them . . .

As I have planted many thousands of natural fruit trees for the good of the common wealth, so also I have taken some spiritual sciences or profits from them. I mean several propositions drawn from observations in nature, which are somewhat branched forth into boughs and twigs, and sent them abroad for the good of the Church of God; and if men will but accept them, and be content to have them engrafted in their own gardens (their hearts and minds) by the Husbandman's watering of them by his Spirit, they will grow and blossom, and bear much good fruit here and for ever. Fruits of faith, love, joy, peace and other fruits of the Spirit, bunches of grapes for the feeding and refreshing of our souls as we travel through the wilderness, and the increase of our glory hereafter in Canaan to all eternity.

RALPH AUSTEN *d.* 1676
The Spiritual Use of an Orchard or Garden of Fruit Trees

8 *Jesus Christ the Apple Tree*

The tree of life my soul hath seen,
Laden with fruit and always green:
The trees of nature fruitless be
Compared with Christ the apple tree.

His beauty doth all things excel:
By faith I know, but ne'er can tell
The glory which I now can see
In Jesus Christ the apple tree.

For happiness I long have sought,
And pleasure dearly I have bought:
I missed of all; but now I see
'Tis found in Christ the apple tree.

I'm weary with my former toil,
Here I will sit and rest awhile:
Under the shadow I will be,
Of Jesus Christ the apple tree.

This fruit doth make my soul to thrive,
It keeps my dying faith alive;
Which makes my soul in haste to be
With Jesus Christ the apple tree.

ANONYMOUS (collection of Joshua Smith 1784)

9 *Splendour in the Flower*

When I was quite a boy, my father used to take me to the
Montpelier Tea-gardens at Walworth. Do I go there now?
No; the place is deserted, and its borders and its beds o'er-
turned. Is there, then, nothing that can

'Bring back the hour
Of glory in the grass, of splendour in the flower?'

Oh! yes. I unlock the casket of memory, and draw back
the warders of the brain; and there this scene of my infant
wanderings still lives unfaded, or with fresher dyes. A new
sense comes upon me, as in a dream; a richer perfume,
brighter colours start out; my eyes dazzle; my heart heaves
with its new load of bliss, and I am a child again. My
sensations are all glossy, spruce, voluptuous, and fine: they
wear a candied coat, and are in holiday trim. I see the beds
of larkspur with purple eyes; tall holy-oaks, red and yellow;
the broad sun-flowers, caked in gold, with bees buzzing

round them; wildernesses of pinks, and hot-glowing pionies; poppies run to seed; the sugared lily, and faint mignionette, all ranged in order, and as thick as they can grow; the box-tree borders; the gravel-walks, the painted alcove, the confectionary, the clotted cream: – I think I see them now with sparkling looks; or have they vanished while I have been writing this description of them? No matter; they will return again when I least think of them. All that I have observed since, of flowers and plants, and grass-plots, and of suburb delights, seems, to me, borrowed from 'that first garden of my innocence' – to be slips and scions stolen from that bed of memory.

WILLIAM HAZLITT 1778–1830 *Table Talk*

10 *Adornment of Nature*

Not surprisingly, as the loveliest adornment of nature, flowers have been made the loveliest adornment of just about everything we have valued. It is not simply that we are a nation of gardeners and a nation of plant-lovers. Love of flowers, and the spiritual value attached to them, is deeply rooted in just about every aspect of our lives. Our language, for example. When we are happy we blossom. A successful enterprise is said to be blooming. A romance that is working out well is flowering. A beautiful woman is as fair as a rose. And so on. Flowers award a stamp of value to what we do and to what we cherish.

The very names we have given to flowers speak of our profoundest affection for them. Woven together they make some of the richest vernacular poetry in our language. Traveller's Joy. Snowdrop. Snapdragon. Pimpernel. Shepherd's Purse. Buttercup. Sweet William. Lily of the Valley. Foxglove. Larkspur. Honeysuckle. Meadowsweet. Periwinkle.

Pennycress. Jack-go-to-bed-at-noon. Columbine. Star of Bethlehem.

What a range of experiences is compressed in that list. They are names that have drawn around themselves, as the flowers themselves have done, veils of folk-lore and meaning. An entire culture of rural life lies in these names: they speak of a human intimacy with nature, a way of life in which a web of countless associations binds people and countryside in harmony. Even when those associations are ugly the poetry is still present. Adderstongue. Viper's Bugloss. Dragon's Teeth. Stinking Hellebore. Fleabane.

As flowers adorn language, so they adorn our sentiments and the places to which our sentiments most deeply attach themselves. If we want to make a house prettier and more loved, then we train flowers over it and plant flowers around it. One of the many unlovable aspects of tower-blocks is the distance imposed from anything that grows. Even the tiniest backyard may have a tub with nasturtiums trailing from it and a buddleia that has crammed itself into the chink of a wall, glimpsing the sun just long enough to attract a butterfly.

EDWIN MULLINS b. 1933 A Love Affair with Nature

11 Flower in the Cannied Wall

'The flower was plucked out of a wall at "Waggoners Wells", near Haslemere' (T)

Flower in the crannied wall,
I pluck you out of the crannies,
I hold you here, root and all, in my hand,
Little flower – but if I could understand
What you are, root and all, and all in all,
I should know what God and man is.

ALFRED TENNYSON 1809–1892

12 *Brave Flowers*

Brave flowers – that I could gallant it like you,
    And be as little vain!
You come abroad, and make a harmless show,
    And to your beds of earth again.
You are not proud: you know your birth:
For your embroidered garments are from earth.

You do obey your months and times, but I
    Would have it ever Spring:
My fate would know no Winter, never die,
    Nor think of such a thing.
O that I could my bed of earth but view
And smile, and look as cheerfully as you!

O teach me to see Death and not to fear,
    But rather to take truce!
How often have I seen you at a bier,
    And there look fresh and spruce!
You fragrant flowers! then teach me, that my breath
Like yours may sweeten and perfume my death.

HENRY KING 1592–1669 British Museum MS. Harl. 6917

13 *Nature's Renewing*

The family of violets arrived freshly sweet in their cool nest
of moss. Your fingers know how to tuck the flowers in for
a safe journey. They are still in the moss, but with their
faces peeping out rather bashfully, making a contrast to
the bold, self-important aspect of the ugly telephone beside
them . . .

The spring is Nature's renewing. Keep your heart turned
to the sun, and let no trial or fight or perplexity draw your

faith aside; and do inquire sometimes how it fares with those you meet. Some, I know, are struggling; their faith is weak, their winters are long, and it ought not to be so. I believe if we talked more about these things to each other it would be an immense help. There would be less doubting and more faith; less of the season of spiritual inertia, and more of the activity of spring; holiness of heart, and so God's favour and blessing, quickening into life and fruitfulness all the best in us.

CATHERINE BRAMWELL-BOOTH 1883–1988 Letter to G

14 Cabbage and God

Red cabbage is another favourite winter standby, and so beautiful to look at, its colour dark as burgundy, and its interior, like those of the pomegranate or the Chinese gooseberry, one of nature's best bits of evidence for the existence of a Creator.

SUSAN HILL b. 1942 The Magic Apple Tree

15 Guns into Onions

Lord Baldwin was speaking at the Astley Horticultural Society's Show, held in the grounds of Astley Hall, his Worcestershire home, at which he presented the prizes.

'One wonders,' he said, 'if there will ever be sufficient sanity in this world between nations, when they will cease to make large guns, and instead will compete against each other in growing the biggest onions. It would be a wiser world and would serve a more useful purpose.'

THE TIMES 2 August 1938

16 *Dung*

In vacant corners, on the hamlet waste,
The ample dunghill's steaming heap be placed;
There many a month fermenting to remain,
Ere thy slow team disperse it o'er the plain.

The prudent farmer all manure provides,
The mire of roads, the mould of hedge-row sides;
For him their mud the stagnant ponds supply;
For him their soil, the stable and the sty.

JOHN SCOTT 1730–1783 'Amoebaean Eclogues'

17 *A Harvest Scene*

Behold –
The *green* fields *yellowing* into corny gold!
White o'er their ranks, an old man half appears,
How hale he looks, tho' hoared with seventy years;
His prospect mounts, slow-paced, he strives to climb,
And seems some ancient monument of time;
Propped o'er his staff the reverend father stands,
And views Heaven's blessings with up-lifted hands;
Gleeful in heart computes the year's increase,
And portions out, in thought, his homely race,
His homely race before, his hopes improve,
And labour in obedience for his love;
Sweepy they cut, then bind the sheafy-grain,
And bend beneath the burthen of the plain;
His cheerful eyes, with silent praises crown
Their toils, and smile at vigour once his own;
Till the mid-sun to second nature's call,
Noon-marks the distant steeple's ivied wall,

Thence warned, he waves his arms, with giddy haste,
The circling summons to a cool repast.

WILLIAM PATTISON 1706–1727

18 *Harvest Festival*

From our seats in the choir we watched the year turn: Christmas, Easter and Whitsun, Rogation Sunday and prayers for
rain, the Church following the plough very close. Harvest
Festival was perhaps the one we liked best, the one that came
nearest home. Then how heavily and abundantly was our
small church loaded; the cream of the valley was used to
decorate it. Everyone brought of his best from field and
garden; and to enter the church on Harvest morning was
like crawling head first into a horn of plenty, a bursting
granary, a vegetable stall, a grotto of bright flowers. The
normally bare walls sprouted leaves and fruit, the altar great
stooks of wheat, and ornamental loaves as big as cartwheels
stood parked by the communion rails. Bunches of grapes,
from the Squire's own vines, hung blue from the lips of the
pulpit. Gigantic and useless marrows abounded, leeks and
onions festooned the pews, there were eggs and butter on
the lectern shelves, the windows were heaped with apples,
and the fat round pillars which divided the church were
skirted with oats and barley.

Almost everyone in the congregation had some hand in
these things. Square-rumped farmers and ploughmen in
chokers, old gardeners and poultry-keepers, they nodded
and pointed and prodded each other to draw attention to
what they had brought. The Church was older than its one
foundation, was as old as man's life on earth.

The seed of these fruits, and the seat of these men, still
came from the same one bowl; confined to this valley and
renewing itself here, it went back to the days of the Ice.

Pride, placation, and the continuity of growth were what we had come to praise. And even where we sang, 'All is safely gathered in', knowing full well that some of Farmer Lusty's corn still lay rotting in the field, the discrepancy didn't seem important.

LAURIE LEE *b.* 1914 *Cider with Rosie*

19 *The Pitcher Plant*

There is a plant in South America called the 'pitcher plant', on the stalk of which, below each leaf, is a little cup-like formation which is always full of water. When it is very small it is full; as it grows larger it is still full; and when it reaches maturity it is full. That illustrates holiness. All that God asks is that the heart should be cleansed from sin and full of love, whether it be the tender heart of the little child with feeble powers of loving, or the full-grown man, or the flaming archangel before the throne.

SAMUEL LOGAN BRENGLE 1860–1936 *The Way of Holiness*

20 *Spiritual Flowers*

Happy is he who opens his heart to you, good Jesus, for you will enter to feed and rest there at noontime. Your coming, Lord, brings the midday of heavenly light to the chaste breast, calming every emotion of the heart with the infusion of divine peace. You strew the bed upon which you lie with spiritual flowers and adornments, so that the soul perceiving your presence and the sweetness of that sudden peace utters with wondrous love a cry of exultation and joy: You are beautiful, my beloved, and comely, our bed is covered with flowers.

AELRED OF RIEVAULX *c.* 1110–1167 *The Spiritual Kiss*

Hymn: Now the Green Blade Riseth

Now the green blade riseth from the buried grain,
Wheat that in dark earth many days has lain;
Love lives again, that with the dead has been:
Love is come again, like wheat that springeth green.

In the grave they laid him, love whom men had slain,
Thinking that never he would wake again,
Laid in the earth like grain that sleeps unseen:
Love is come again, like wheat that springeth green.

Forth he came at Easter, like the risen grain,
He that for three days in the grave had lain,
Quick from the dead my risen Lord is seen:
Love is come again, like wheat that springeth green.

When our hearts are wintry, grieving, or in pain,
Thy touch can call us back to life again,
Fields of our hearts that dead and bare have been:
Love is come again, like wheat that springeth green.

                              J. M. C. CRUM 1872–1958

7

LET BIRDS FLY ABOVE THE EARTH

Lord, creator of the eagle and the sparrow, the dove and the humming bird, we praise and thank you for the varied beauty of birds, their songs and their flight. Help us to care for this marvellous part of your creation; for your name's sake.

MARLBOROUGH COLLEGE

And it came to pass at the end of forty days, that Noah opened the window of the ark which he had made: and he sent forth a raven, which went forth to and fro, until the waters were dried up from off the earth. Also he sent forth a dove from him, to see if the waters were abated from off the face of the ground; but the dove found no rest for the sole of her foot, and she returned unto him into the ark, for the waters were on the face of the whole earth: then he put forth his hand, and took her, and pulled her in unto him into the ark. And he stayed yet other seven days; and again he sent forth the dove out of the ark; and the dove came in to him in the evening; and, lo, in her mouth was an olive leaf plucked off: so Noah knew that the waters were abated from off the earth.

GENESIS 8: 6–11

And Jesus, when he was baptized, went up straightway out of the water: and, lo, the heavens were opened unto him, and he saw the Spirit of God descending like a dove, and lighting upon him: and lo a voice from heaven, saying, This is my beloved Son, in whom I am well pleased.

MATTHEW 3: 16–17

1 *The Mass of the Birds*

This morning, lying couched amid the grass
In the deep, deep dingle south of Llangwyth's Pass,
  While it was yet neither quite bright nor dark,
I heard a new and wonderful High Mass.
  The Chief Priest was the nightingale, the lark
And thrush assisted him, and some small bird
  (I do not weet his name) acted as Clerk.
My spirit was lapped in ecstasy: each word,
Word after word, thrilled through me like the deep
Rich music of a dream; not wholly asleep
Nor all awake was I, but, as it were,
  Tranced somewhere between one state and the other.
  All heavy thoughts that through the long day smother
Man's heart and soul with weariness and care
  Were gone, and in their place reigned pure delight.
  The nightingale, sent from a far and bright
Land by my golden sister, prophesied
  Of blessèd days to come, in a sweet voice;
  And the small bird, responding, sang 'Rejoice, rejoice!'
I heard his little bill tinkle and jingle
With a clear silver sound that filled the dingle.
Heaven is a state wherein bliss and devotion mingle,
  And such was mine this morn: I could have died
Of rapture! Never knelt upon his hassock
  Bishop or deacon with a holier feeling.
How beautifully shone the thrush's cassock,
  Covered all over with a thousand strange
  And lovely flowers, like those upon an Arabesque ceiling!
The altar seemed of such resplendent gold
  As no man, even a miser, would exchange
For all the jewels in the East of old.
Two hours I lay admiring all I saw,
  Yet those two hours appeared to me no more

Than as a moment; I look back with awe
And wonder at what then I thought and felt,
  And would give all my fame, and all my love,
    Yea, even almost my life, but to restore
The rapturous emotions that then dwelt
  Within my bosom! Ah! this may not be –
But glory unto God, who in his infinite love
  Created Man to enjoy to eternity
Even greater happiness in his own Heaven above!

DAFYDD AP GWILYM 1340–1370

2 A Fragment of Melody

The mist has cleared, and the sun is shining with a luminous warmth that makes the whole island glisten with the splendour of a gem, and fills the sea and sky with a radiance of blue light.

I have come out to lie on the rocks where I have the black edge of the north island in front of me, Galway Bay, too blue almost to look at, on my right, the Atlantic on my left, a perpendicular cliff under my ankles, and over me innumerable gulls that chase each other in a white cirrus of wings.

A nest of hooded crows is somewhere near me, and one of the old birds is trying to drive me away by letting itself fall like a stone every few moments, from about forty yards above me to within reach of my hand.

Gannets are passing up and down above the sound, swooping at times after a mackerel, and further off I can see the whole fleet of hookers coming out from Kilronan for a night's fishing in the deep water to the west.

As I lie here hour after hour, I seem to enter into the wild pastimes of the cliff, and to become a companion of the cormorants and crows.

Many of the birds display themselves before me with the vanity of barbarians, forming in strange evolutions as long as I am in sight, and returning to their ledge of rock when I am gone. Some are wonderfully expert, and cut graceful figures for an inconceivable time without a flap of their wings, growing so absorbed in their own dexterity that they often collide with one another in their flight, an incident always followed by a wild outburst of abuse. Their language is easier than Gaelic, and I seem to understand the greater part of their cries, though I am not able to answer. There is one plaintive note which they take up in the middle of their usual babble with extraordinary effect, and pass on from one to another along the cliff with a sort of an inarticulate wail, as if they remembered for an instant the horror of the mist.

On the low sheets of rock to the east I can see a number of red and grey figures hurrying about their work. The continual passing in this island between the misery of last night and the splendour of to-day, seems to create an affinity between the moods of these people and the moods of varying rapture and dismay that are frequent in artists, and in certain forms of alienation. Yet it is only in the intonation of a few sentences or some old fragment of melody that I catch the real spirit of the island, for in general the men sit together and talk with endless iteration of the tides and fish, and of the price of kelp in Connemara.

JOHN SYNGE 1871–1909 *The Aran Islands*

3 *I Saw Birds*

I saw birds in the bushes building their nests,
Which man, for all his wit, could never make.
I wondered who taught the magpie how to place the twigs
On which she lays her eggs and breeds her young.
No craftsman could fashion such a nest;

And it would be a marvel if a mason could construct a
    mould for it.

Even more I wondered at the other birds
Who conceal and cover their eggs secretly
On moors and marshes, so that men never find them;
And who hide them more carefully still when they go
    away,
To conceal them from animals and birds of prey.
And I noticed some birds who tread their mates
And bring forth their young high above the ground,
While others conceive at their beaks while breathing.
And I saw the way that peacocks breed.
And seeing these things I wondered at their master,
Who taught them to build their nests so high in the trees,
Where neither man nor beast may reach their young.

WILLIAM LANGLAND *c.* 1332–1400 *Piers the Ploughman*

4 *Indescribable Sweetness*

Now as has already been written there were in the Garden
many beautiful birds and their voices mingled together so
that no one might ever perceive from which bird each song
came, yet the whole melody was of indescribable sweetness.

Among all these birds there was only one which had no
beauty. It was small and brown and looked like a pebble in
a casket of jewels. So it seemed to the Disciple like a wedding
guest who had put on no wedding garment for the sake of
the Beloved. Therefore he was very angry for the Beloved's
sake and drove the bird from the Garden.

But no sooner had it flown out than, although all the other
birds still sang melodiously, the song of the Garden seemed
to have lost its sweetness and the lovely roses in the Garden
dropped their heads and began to die.

At once the Lover came out and asked the Disciple what had become of the brown bird.

The Disciple was amazed and told the Lover all that had happened.

Whereon the Lover went swiftly out of the Garden and called the brown bird which came flying and perched on his shoulder. So he brought it into the Garden again and it sang joyously because it had returned to the Garden. Thereupon the whole Garden was filled with melody and the roses lifted their heads again.

Then the Disciple asked the Lover, 'Sir, please tell me what bird this is and how did you perceive at once that it was absent from the Garden?'

The Lover replied, 'It is called the nightingale and by as much as its plumage is less beautiful than that of the other birds, by that much its voice is sweeter and louder than all of theirs, so that it fills all the Garden with melody, and so beautiful is its song that when the roses no longer hear it they drop their heads.'

So the Disciple perceived that each thing has its own gifts to bring to the service of the Beloved.

ROBERT WAY *b.* 1912 *The Garden of the Beloved*

5 *The White Birds*

I would that we were, my beloved, white birds on the
     foam of the sea!
We tire of the flame of the meteor, before it can fade and
     flee:
And the flame of the blue star of twilight, hung low on the
     rim of the sky,
Has awaked in our hearts, my beloved, a sadness that may
     not die.

A weariness comes from those dreamers, dew dabbled, the
    lily and rose;
Ah, dream not of them, my beloved, the flame of the
    meteor that goes,
Or the flame of the blue star that lingers hung low in the
    fall of the dew:
For I would we were changed to white birds on the
    wandering foam: I and you!

I am haunted by numberless islands, and many a Danaan
    shore,
Where Time would surely forget us, and Sorrow come near
    us no more;
Soon far from the rose and the lily, and fret of the flames
    would we be,
Were we only white birds, my beloved, buoyed out on the
    foam of the sea!

WILLIAM BUTLER YEATS 1865–1939

6 *Upon the Swallow*

This pretty bird, oh, how she flies and sings!
But could she do so if she had not wings?
Her wings bespeak my faith, her songs my peace;
When I believe and sing, my doubtings cease.

JOHN BUNYAN 1628–1688

7 *The Skylark*

Bird of the wilderness,
Blithesome and cumberless,
Sweet be thy matin o'er moorland and lea!
Emblem of happiness,

Blest is thy dwelling-place –
O to abide in the desert with thee!
   Wild is thy lay and loud,
   Far in the downy cloud,
Love gives it energy, love gave it birth.
   Where, on thy dewy wing,
   Where art thou journeying?
Thy lay is in heaven, thy love is on earth.

   O'er fell and mountain sheen,
   O'er moor and mountain green,
O'er the red streamer that heralds the day,
   Over the cloudlet dim,
   Over the rainbow's rim,
Musical cherub, soar, singing, away!
   Then, when the gloaming comes,
   Low in the heather blooms
Sweet will thy welcome and bed of love be!
   Emblem of happiness,
   Blest is thy dwelling-place –
O to abide in the desert with thee!

JAMES HOGG 1770–1835

8 *The Robin's Song*

God bless the field and bless the furrow,
Stream and branch and rabbit burrow,
Hill and stone and flower and tree,
From Bristol town to Wetherby –
Bless the sun and bless the sleet,
Bless the lane and bless the street,
Bless the night and bless the day,
From Somerset and all the way
To the meadows of Cathay;
Bless the minnow, bless the whale,

Bless the rainbow and the hail,
Bless the nest and bless the leaf,
Bless the righteous and the thief,
Bless the wing and the fin,
Bless the air I travel in,
Bless the mill and bless the mouse,
Bless the miller's bricken house,
Bless the earth and bless the sea,
God bless you and God bless me.

ANONYMOUS An Old English Song

9 Bird Worship

The evening proceedings and manœuvres of the rooks are curious and amusing in the autumn. Just before dusk they return in long strings from the foraging of the day, and rendezvous by thousands over *Selborne-down*, where they wheel round in the air, and sport and dive in a playful manner, all the while exerting their voices, and making a loud cawing, which, being blended and softened by the distance that we at the village are below them, becomes a confused noise or chiding; or rather a pleasing murmur, very engaging to the imagination, and not unlike the cry of a pack of hounds in hollow echoing woods, or the rushing of the wind in tall trees, or the tumbling of the tide upon a pebbly shore. When this ceremony is over, with the last gleam of day, they retire for the night to the deep beechen woods of *Tisted* and *Ropley*. We remember a little girl who, as she was going to bed, used to remark on such an occurrence, in the true spirit of *physico-theology*, that the rooks were saying their prayers; and yet this child was much too young to be aware that the scriptures have said of the Deity, that 'he feedeth the ravens who call upon him'.

GILBERT WHITE 1720–1793 *The Natural History of Selborne*

10 *Now Came the Owls*

And now came the owls. They had nested in the garden-side elms, and their young made a curious sound all day, but especially towards evening, as of a person breathing heavily in sleep. At twilight, as we sat still before our house, they came down upon the grass, two big brown owls and three fledglings. Every evening at the same hour they would come, and there would be flying instructions from the elders. They often had the greatest difficulty in making the young ones pay attention, though. One of the parents would fly a little way, then alight and look back for the others to follow. But all their backs were turned. So she returned and did her flight again and again, until they condescended to observe her, and one would be moved to raise its wings and give a compunctious hop. Whereupon the other two would hop. Then all three would hop, and turn and stand looking in the other direction again. This while the father-bird (surely it was the father) stood magisterially on a log observing the progress of the instruction. The mother was indefatigable. 'See, this is the way to do it. Like this. Oh, you aren't paying attention. Do please look. Now watch me. There. Now try. Oh, you can do much better than that if you like. See, like this.'

She alighted on the log near papa, who shook his feathers and seemed to recollect himself. 'Asleep, my dear? Nonsense. I was watching attentively.' He hopped down and joined the three recalcitrants. 'Now, children, you really must pay attention to your mother. You are getting of an age when you can expect to be beak-fed no longer. You must seriously begin to equip yourselves for going out into the world and earning your own living.'

The mother had now recovered her breath and started fluttering before them again. They dutifully fluttered after her, while father strutted pompously back to his log.

Soon, however, the young ones were infected with the flying craze and all the parents did was to stand while the three flew from bough to bough and tree to tree about their heads. Then one day they were gone, parents and all.

ADRIAN BELL 1901–1980 *The Cherry Tree*

11 *A Kind of Magic*

The snow goose had taken flight, her giant wings spread, but she was flying low, and once came quite close to them, so that for a moment the spreading black-tipped, white pinions seemed to caress them and they felt the rush of the bird's swift passage. Once, twice, she circled the lighthouse, then dropped to earth again in the enclosure with the pinioned geese and commenced to feed.

'She be'ent going,' said Frith, with marvel in her voice. The bird in its close passage seemed to have woven a kind of magic about her. 'The Princess be goin' t' stay.'

'Ay,' said Rhayader, and his voice was shaken too. 'She'll stay. She will never go away again. The Lost Princess is lost no more. This is her home now – of her own free will.'

PAUL GALLICO 1897–1976 *The Snow Goose*

12 *A Special Morning*

At night the trees seemed to creep round the house, and the blackbirds never ceased their flutings and their startled chuckles and chuggings among the bushes till the first stars came out over the hill. When at last they were silent the young owls hissed softly to each other on the beeches by the nursery window.

There was never such a place for birds. With the turn of the year the ploughed fields were white with gulls that bred near one of the mountain lakes; early in April the curlews came inland with their desolate cry which Delia's quick ears were always the first to catch, and the rooks clamoured and argued over their nests, breaking off twigs from the trees with a sideways wrench of their strong beaks, and walking mincingly on the lawn as they searched for moss.

Every year the house-martins built their nests outside Delia's and Lucy's bedroom window, and the drenched spring fields, where pools of rain-water winked with a thousand eyes, were full of tumbling, calling peewits. The pretty nut-hatches ran up and down the tree-trunks and the woodpeckers' rat-tat-tat echoed all day. They with their hammer and the great tits with their harsh sawing were as noisy as a carpenter's shop.

Along the river bank there were moor-hens, always engaged on some bustling business of their own, graceful dippers and water-wagtails, and the brilliant, shy kingfishers, while sometimes a heron stood pensively fishing, or winged his sulky flight to the remote and reedy haunts of the wild duck.

One morning something woke Lucy very early before it was quite light. While she lay still in bed one small, sleepy bird piped a note, another answered, and thereupon there burst out such a clamour of voices, such an urgency of song that this seemed to be no ordinary daybreak, but one made above all others for gladness and rejoicing. After that Lucy fell asleep and did not wake until Louisa came in to say it was past seven.

When Lucy told Delia about the birds she said they sang like that every morning – she had often heard them; nor was the day that followed in any way unusual. But Lucy never forgot the first time she heard them; she was certain it was a special morning. Perhaps, she reflected, no day was really ordinary; it was always meant to be new and exciting – if only one did not spoil it all.

EILUNED LEWIS 1900–1979 *Dew on the Grass*

13 *Bell-birds*

By channels of coolness the echoes are calling,
And down the dim gorges I hear the creek falling:
It lives in the mountain where moss and the sedges
Touch with their beauty the banks and the ledges.
Through breaks of the cedar and sycamore bowers
Struggles the light that is love to the flowers;
And, softer than slumber, and sweeter than singing,
The notes of the bell-birds are running and ringing.

The silver-voiced bell-birds, the darlings of daytime!
They sing in September their songs of the May-time;
When shadows wax strong, and the thunder-bolts hurtle,
They hide with their fear in the leaves of the myrtle;
When rain and the sunbeams shine mingled together,
They start up like fairies that follow fair weather;
And straightway the hues of their feathers unfolden
Are the green and the purple, the blue and the golden.

October, the maiden of bright yellow tresses,
Loiters for love in these cool wildernesses;
Loiters, knee-deep, in the grasses, to listen,
Where dripping rocks gleam and the leafy pools glisten:
Then is the time when the water-moons splendid
Break with their gold, and are scattered or blended
Over the creeks, till the woodlands have warning
Of songs of the bell-bird and wings of the Morning.

Welcome as waters unkissed by the summers
Are the voices of bell-birds to thirsty far-comers.
When fiery December sets foot in the forest,
And the need of the wayfarer presses the sorest,
Pent in the ridges for ever and ever
The bell-birds direct him to spring and to river,
With ring and with ripple, like runnels whose torrents
Are toned by the pebbles and leaves in the currents.

Often I sit, looking back to a childhood,
Mixt with the sights and the sounds of the wildwood,
Longing for power and the sweetness to fashion,
Lyrics with beats like the heart-beats of Passion; –
Songs interwoven of lights and of laughters
Borrowed from bell-birds in far forest-rafters;
So I might keep in the city and alleys
The beauty and strength of the deep mountain valleys:
Charming to slumber the pain of my losses
With glimpses of creeks and a vision of mosses.

HENRY KENDALL 1839–1882

14 *Four Ducks on a Pond*

Four ducks on a pond,
A grass-bank beyond,
A blue sky of spring,
White clouds on the wing;
What a little thing
To remember for years –
To remember with tears!

WILLIAM ALLINGHAM 1824–1889

15 *The Silver Swan*

The silver swan, who living had no note,
When death approached, unlocked her silent throat,
Leaning her breast against the reedy shore,
Thus sung her first and last, and sung no more:
'Farewell all joys! O death, come close mine eyes;
More geese than swans now live, more fools than wise.'

ORLANDO GIBBONS 1583–1625

16 *Grip*

'Mother,' he said, after a long silence, 'how long, how many days and nights – shall I be kept here?'

'Not many, dear, I hope not many.'

'You hope! Ay, but your hoping will not undo these chains. Grip hopes, but who cares for Grip?'

The raven gave a short, dull melancholy croak. It said 'Nobody', as plain as a croak could speak.

'Who cares for Grip, except you and me?' said Barnaby, smoothing the bird's rumpled feathers with his hand. 'He never speaks in this place; he never says a word in jail; he sits and mopes all day in his dark corner, dozing sometimes, and sometimes looking at the light that creeps in through the bars, and shines in his bright eye, as if a spark from those great fires had fallen into the room and was burning yet. But who cares for Grip?'

The raven croaked again – Nobody.

'And by the way,' said Barnaby, withdrawing his hand from the bird and laying it upon his mother's arm, as he looked eagerly in her face; 'if they kill me – they may: I heard it said they would – what will become of Grip when I am dead?'

The sound of the word, or the current of his own thoughts, suggested to Grip his own phrase, 'Never say die!' But he stopped short in the middle of it, drew a dismal cork, and subsided into a faint croak, as if he lacked the heart to get through the shortest sentence.

CHARLES DICKENS 1812–1870 Barnaby Rudge

17 *I sometimes think I'd rather crow*

I sometimes think I'd rather crow
And be a rooster than to roost
And be a crow. But I dunno.

A rooster he can roost also,
Which don't seem fair when crows can't crow.
Which may help some. Still I dunno.

Crows should be glad of one thing though;
Nobody thinks of eating crow,
While roosters they are good enough
For anyone unless they're tough.

There're lots of tough old roosters though,
And anyway a crow can't crow,
So mebby roosters stand more show.
It looks that way. But I dunno.

ANONYMOUS

18 *A Parrot Named Pete*

i got acquainted with
a parrot named pete recently
who is an interesting bird
pete says he used
to belong to the fellow
that ran the mermaid tavern
in london then i said
you must have known
shakespeare know him said pete
poor mutt i knew him well
he called me pete and i called him
bill but why do you say poor mutt

well said pete bill was a
disappointed man and was always
boring his friends about what
he might have been and done
if he only had a fair break
two or three pints of sack
and sherris and the tears
would trickle down into his
beard and his beard would get
soppy and wilt his collar

DON MARQUIS 1878–1937 'pete the parrot and shakespeare'

19 *The Old Sweet Dove of Wiveton*

'Twas the voice of the sweet dove
I heard him move
I heard him cry
Love, love.

High in the chestnut tree
Is the nest of the old dove
And there he sits solitary
Crying, Love, love.

The gray of this heavy day
Makes the green of the trees' leaves and the grass brighter
And the flowers of the chestnut tree whiter
And whiter the flowers of the high cow-parsley.

So still is the air
So heavy the sky
You can hear the splash
Of the water falling from the green grass
As Red and Honey push by,
The old dogs,
Gone away, gone hunting by the marsh bogs.

Happy the retriever dogs in their pursuit
Happy in bog-mud the busy foot.

Now all is silent, it is silent again
In the sombre day and the beginning soft rain
It is a silence made more actual
By the moan from the high tree that is occasional,
Where in his nest above
Still sits the old dove,
Murmuring solitary
Crying for pain,
Crying most melancholy
Again and again.

STEVIE SMITH 1902–1971

20 *A Blackbird Singing*

It seems wrong that out of this bird,
Black, bold, a suggestion of dark
Places about it, there yet should come
Such rich music, as though the notes'
Ore were changed to a rare metal
At one touch of that bright bill.

You have heard it often, alone at your desk
In a green April, your mind drawn
Away from its work by sweet disturbance
Of the mild evening outside your room.

A slow singer, but loading each phrase
With history's overtones, love, joy
And grief learned by his dark tribe
In other orchards and passed on
Instinctively as they are now,
But fresh always with new tears.

R. S. THOMAS *b.* 1913

Hymn: Yes, God is Good

Yes, God is good – in earth and sky,
From ocean-depths and spreading wood,
Ten thousand voices seem to cry:
'God made us all, and God is good'.

The sun that keeps his trackless way
And downward pours his golden flood,
Night's sparkling hosts, all seem to say
In accents clear that God is good.

The merry birds prolong the strain,
Their song with every spring renewed;
And balmy air and falling rain,
Each softly whispers: 'God is good'.

We hear it in the rushing breeze;
The hills that have for ages stood,
The echoing sky and roaring seas,
All swell the chorus: 'God is good'.

For all thy gifts we bless thee, Lord,
But chiefly for our heavenly food,
Thy pardoning grace, thy quickening word,
These prompt our song, that God is good.

JOHN HAMPDEN GURNEY 1802–1862

8

LET THE EARTH PUT FORTH ANIMALS

O Lord Jesus Christ, who has taught us that without our Father in heaven no sparrow falls to the ground, help us to be very kind to all animals, and our pets. May we remember that thou wilt one day ask us if we have been good to them. Bless us as we take care of them; for thy sake.

ANONYMOUS

The wolf also shall dwell with the lamb, and the leopard shall lie down with the kid; and the calf and the young lion and the fatling together; and a little child shall lead them. And the cow and the bear shall feed; their young ones shall lie down together: and the lion shall eat straw like the ox. And the sucking child shall play on the hole of the asp, and the weaned child shall put his hand on the cockatrice' den. They shall not hurt nor destroy in all my holy mountain: for the earth shall be full of the knowledge of the Lord, as the waters cover the sea.

ISAIAH 11:6–9

What man of you, having an hundred sheep, if he lose one of them, doth not leave the ninety and nine in the wilderness, and go after that which is lost, until he find it? And when he hath found it, he layeth it on his shoulders, rejoicing. And when he cometh home, he calleth together his friends and neighbours, saying unto them, Rejoice with me; for I have found my sheep which was lost.

I say unto you, that likewise joy shall be in heaven over one sinner that repenteth, more than over ninety and nine just persons, which need no repentance.

LUKE 15:4–7

1 *A Dream of Animals*

I have had many dreams about animals, domestic, wild, and legendary, but I shall describe only one at this point, as it seems to me to throw into an imaginative shape two of the things I have been writing about: our relation to the animal world, a relation involving a predestined guilt, and our immortality. All guilt seeks expiation and the end of guilt, and our blood-guiltiness towards the animals tries to find release in visions of a day when man and the beasts will live in friendship and the lion will lie down with the lamb. My dream was connected with this vision. I dreamed that I was lying asleep, when a light in my room wakened me. A man was standing by my bedside. He was wearing a long robe, which fell about him in motionless folds, while he stood like a column. The light that filled the room came from his hair, which rose straight up from his head, burning, like a motionless brazier. He raised his hand, and without touching me, merely by making that sign, lifted me to my feet in one movement, so that I stood before him. He turned and went out through the door, and I followed him. We were in the gallery of a cloister; the moon was shining, and the shadows of arches made black ribs on the flagstones. We went through a street, at the end of which there was a field, and while we walked on the moonlight changed to the white light of early morning. As we passed the last houses I saw a dark, shabby man with a dagger in his hand; he was wearing rags bound round his feet, so that he walked quite soundlessly; there was a stain as of blood on one of his sleeves; I took him to be a robber or a murderer and was afraid. But as he came nearer I saw that his eyes, which were fixed immovably on the figure beside me, were filled with a profound, violent adoration such as I had never seen in human eyes before. Then, behind him, I caught sight of a confused crowd of other men and women in curious or ragged clothes, and all had their eyes fixed with the same look on the man walking beside me. I saw their faces only for a moment. Presently we came to the field, which as we drew near changed into a great plain dotted with little conical hills a little higher than a man's head. All over the plain animals were standing or sitting on their haunches on these little hills; lions, tigers, bulls, deer, elephants, were there; serpents too wreathed their lengths on the knolls; and each was separate and alone, and each slowly lifted its head upward as if in prayer. This upward-lifting motion had a strange solemnity and deliberation; I watched head after head upraised as if proclaiming some truth just realized, and yet as if moved by an irresistible power beyond them. The elephant wreathed its trunk upward, and there was something pathetic and absurd in that indirect act of adoration. But the other animals raised their heads with the inevitability of the sun's rising, as if they knew, like the sun, that a new day was about to begin, and were giving the signal for its coming. Then I saw a little dog busily running about with his nose tied to the ground, as if he did not know that the animals had been redeemed. He was a friendly little dog, officiously going about his business, and it seemed to me that he too had a place in this day, and that his oblivious concern with the earth was also a sort of worship. How the dream ended I do not remember: I have now only a memory of the great animals with all their heads raised to heaven.

EDWIN MUIR 1887–1959 *An Autobiography*

2 *Sacred Symbols*

We must remember that primitive man was far closer to the animals than we can imagine. Indeed, he felt, with good reason, that the animals were his superiors. This seems to me to be the message of the early wall-paintings, like those at Lascaux. The few men who appear on the uneven walls of Lascaux cut very poor figures compared to the vigorous animals. Can we seriously believe that these wretched little creatures thought that, by representing their magnificent companions, they were gaining power over them? Are they not, rather, expressing their envy and admiration? . . .

The next stage in man's relationship with animals, is the choice of an animal as the sacred symbol of a group; what is loosely called a totem. Hunting for their necessary food; and admiring to the point of worship a life-endowment greater than their own; there was thus established from the earliest times a dual relationship that has persisted to the present day: love and worship, enmity and fear.

KENNETH CLARK 1903–1983 *Animals and Men*

3 *The Mouse's Petition*

Found in the trap, where he had been confined all night

O hear a pensive prisoner's prayer,
    For liberty that sighs;
And never let thine heart be shut
    Against the wretch's cries!

For here forlorn and sad I sit
    Within the wiry grate;
And tremble at the approaching morn,
    Which brings impending fate.

If e'er thy breast with freedom glowed
    And spurned a tyrant's chain,
Let not thy strong oppressive force
    A free-born mouse detain.

O do not stain with guiltless blood
    Thy hospitable hearth;

Nor triumph that thy wiles betrayed
  A prize so little worth!

The scattered gleanings of a feast
  My frugal meals supply:
But if thine unrelenting heart
  That slender boon deny,

The cheerful light, the vital air,
  Are blessings widely given;
Let nature's commoners enjoy
  The common gifts of heaven.

ANNA LAETITIA BARBAULD 1743–1825

4 *The Grey Squirrel*

Like a small grey
coffee-pot,
sits the squirrel.
He is not

all he should be,
kills by dozens
trees, and eats
his red-brown cousins.

The keeper on the
other hand,
who shot him, is
a Christian, and

loves his enemies.
Which shows
the squirrel was not
one of those.

HUMBERT WOLFE 1885–1940

5 *Animal Love*

With regard to animals – even with respect to our dogs that
we know and love best, we are often in the dark as to what
is their momentary disposition and requirements. But how
instructive it is to watch precisely such animals thus dear to
us – I mean their knowledge and love of us, and their need
of us and of our love. Our dogs know us and love us, human
individuals, from amongst millions of fairly similar other
individuals. Our dogs know us and love us thus most really,
yet they doubtless know us only vividly, not clearly; we
evidently strain their minds after a while – they then like to
get away amongst servants and children; and, indeed, they
love altogether to escape from human company, the rich and
dim, or (at best) the vivid experiences – the company that
is above them, to the company of their fellow-creatures, the
company that affords so much poorer but so much clearer
impressions – the level company of their brother-dogs. And
yet, how wonderful! dogs thus require their fellow-dogs,
the shallow and clear, but they also require us, the deep and
dim; they require indeed what they can grasp; but they as
really require what they can but reach out to, more or less
– what exceeds, protects, envelops, directs them. And, after
a short relaxation in the dog-world, they return to the
bracing of the man-world.

FRIEDRICH VON HÜGEL 1852–1925 *Essays and Addresses*

6 *Moving Ears*

Every morning, after Jody had curried and brushed the pony,
he let down the barrier of the stall, and Gabilan thrust past
him and raced down the barn and into the corral. Around
and around he galloped, and sometimes he jumped forward

and landed on stiff legs. He stood quivering, stiff ears forward, eyes rolling so that the whites showed, pretending to be frightened. At last he walked snorting to the water-trough and buried his nose in the water up to the nostrils. Jody was proud then, for he knew that was the way to judge a horse. Poor horses only touched their lips to the water, but a fine spirited beast put his whole nose and mouth under, and only left room to breathe.

Then Jody stood and watched the pony, and he saw things he had never noticed about any other horse, the sleek, sliding flank muscles and the cords of the buttocks, which flexed like a closing fist, and the shine the sun put on the red coat. Having seen horses all his life, Jody had never looked at them very closely before. But now he noticed the moving ears which gave expression and even inflection of expression to the face. The pony talked with his ears. You could tell exactly how he felt about everything by the way his ears pointed. Sometimes they were stiff and upright and sometimes lax and sagging. They went back when he was angry or fearful, and forward when he was anxious and curious and pleased; and their exact position indicated which emotion he had.

JOHN STEINBECK 1902–1968 *The Red Pony*

7 *The Toad*

With solemn hampered pace proceeding by
    The dewy garden-bed,
Like some old priest in antique finery,
    Stiff cope and jewelled head;

Thy sanctuary lamps are lit at dusk,
    Where leafy aisles are dim;
The bat's shrill piccolo, the swinging musk
    Blend with the beetle's hymn.

Aye something paramount and priestly too,
  Some cynic mystery,
Lurks in the dull skin with its dismal hue,
  The bright ascetic eye;

Thy heaving throat, thy sick repulsive glance
  Still awes thy foes around;
The eager hound starts back and looks askance,
  And whining paws the ground.

Yet thou has forfeited thy ancient ban,
  Thy mystical control;
We know thee now to be the friend of man,
  A simple homely soul;

And when we deemed thee curiously wise,
  Still chewing venomed paste,
Thou didst but crush the limbs of juicy flies
  With calm and critic taste.

A. C. BENSON 1862–1925

8 *The Hermit and the Fox*

When Piran first arrived in Cornwall, he sat down under a
tree; and lying under the same tree was a wild boar. At first,
on seeing Piran, the boar fled in terror. But then, sensing
Piran's great love for all God's creatures, the boar became
tame, and returned to Piran to become his servant. He thus
became Piran's first monk. The boar began to tear branches
and grass with his teeth, and built Piran a simple cell in
which to live. And soon other animals came out of the forest
to join Piran and the boar: a fox, a badger, a wolf and a doe.
They were all quite tame, obeying Piran as their abbot.

  One day the fox, who was more crafty than the other
animals, stole Piran's shoes; and, abandoning his intention

to live as a monk, he carried them to his old lair in the forest, to chew them there. Piran, when he realised what had happened, sent the badger after the fox, to persuade him to return to the monastery. So the badger, who knew the forest well, went straight to the fox's lair; and, seeing the fox about to eat his master's shoes, bit his ears and tail. Then, with his teeth in the fox's fur, the badger pulled the fox back to the monastery.

When the fox arrived, Piran asked him: 'Why have you committed this crime, dear brother – something that a monk should never do? Look, we all share the same sweet water and the same food. And if you had craved meat, according to your nature, God would have turned the bark of this tree into meat for you.' The fox begged Piran's forgiveness, and did penance by fasting, refusing to eat until Piran gave permission.

And from then onwards all the animals lived in peace, bound together by devotion to their abbot.

ANONYMOUS (Celtic)

9 *The Hermit and the Bear*

Thus prayed Florens by his bed,
He prayed dear God of him take heed;
And rising up and looking out
He saw a bear, wild and stout.
This bear he came unto the gate,
He came to where Florens he sat,
And when the bear he came him near
The bear him louted and made fair cheer;
Such fair cheer as a bear might make
And asked meek he would him take.
At this Florens him bethought
That God had heard what he besought

And thanked him of his sweet grace
That he had sent him such solace,
For a miracle he must understand
That a wild bear came so tame to hand.
Now Florens he had six sheep
But no herdsman them to keep,
So bade the bear that he should go
And drive his sheep to and fro.
'And keep them well that none them tear
And thou shalt be my good bear.'
The bear him louted with semblance glad
For to do what Florens bade,
So to the bear he gave advice:
'Every day when I eat twice
Come thou home at high undurne
And no longer in the field sojourn!
And every day when I fast
At the nones come home at last.'
So did the bear every day,
Ne'er one hour passed he away,
But came he home unto the cell
Always at both times he knew well.
Then Florens had comfort and gain
Of his bear that was so tame,
And loved him much without fail
For the miracle and the marvel.
And, sooth to say, to him appeared
The bear was a most marvellous herd.
A bear through kind should eat sheep
Yet here as herd he did them keep,
And the miracle might not be hid
The whole country knew it was did:
That Florens had a tame bear
That of his sheep the herdsman were.

ANONYMOUS (Medieval) 'The Marvellous Bear Shepherd'

10 *The Great Open Spaces*

'If I had my way, Stubbins, there wouldn't be a single lion or tiger in captivity anywhere in the world. They never take to it. They're never happy. They never settle down. They are always thinking of the big countries they have left behind. You can see it in their eyes, dreaming – dreaming always of the great open spaces where they were born; dreaming of the deep, dark jungles where their mothers first taught them how to scent and track the deer. And what are they given in exchange for all this?' asked the Doctor, stopping in his walk and growing all red and angry – 'What are they given in exchange for the glory of an African sunrise, for the twilight breeze whispering through the palms, for the green shade of the matted, tangled vines, for the cool, big-starred nights of the desert, for the patter of the waterfall after a hard day's hunt? What, I ask you are they given in exchange for *these*? Why, a bare cage with iron bars; an ugly piece of dead meat thrust in to them once a day, and a crowd of fools to come and stare at them with open mouths! – No, Stubbins. Lions and tigers, the Big Hunters, should never, never be seen in zoos.'

HUGH LOFTING 1886–1947 *The Voyages of Doctor Doolittle*

11 *A Sudden Eruption*

I was just about to turn my attention to the butterfly again when I saw something that I could hardly believe: the patch of earth I had been looking at suddenly heaved upwards, as though pushed by a hand from beneath; the soil cracked and a tiny seedling waved about wildly before its pale roots gave way and it fell on its side.

What, I wondered, could be the cause of this sudden

eruption? An earthquake? Surely not so small and confined. A mole? Not in such dry and waterless terrain. As I was speculating, the earth gave another heave, clods of it cracked off and rolled away, and I was looking at a brown and yellow shell. More earth was swept out of the way as the shell bucked upwards, and then, slowly and cautiously, a wrinkled, scaly head appeared out of the hole, a long, skinny neck followed it. The bleary eyes blinked once or twice as the tortoise surveyed me; then, deciding I must be harmless, he hoisted himself with infinite care and effort out of his earth cell, walked two or three steps, and sank down in the sunshine, drowsing gently. After the long winter under the damp and chilly soil, that first sun-bath must have been like a drink of wine to the reptile. His legs were spread out from his shell, his neck extended as far as it could, his head resting on the ground; with eyes closed, the creature seemed to be absorbing sunshine through every bit of his body and shell. He remained lying there for about ten minutes, and then he rose, slowly and deliberately, and rolled off down the path to where a patch of dandelion and clover spread in the shade of a cypress. Here his legs seemed to give way and he collapsed on to the bottom of his shell with a thump. Then his head appeared from his shell, bent slowly down towards the rich green pile of the clover patch, his mouth opened wide, there was a moment's suspense, and then his mouth closed round the succulent leaves, his head jerked back to tear them off and he sat there munching happily, his mouth stained with the first food of the year.

GERALD DURRELL *b.* 1925 *My Family and Other Animals*

12 *The Kangaroo*

Kangaroo, Kangaroo!
Thou Spirit of Australia,
That redeems from utter failure,
From perfect desolation,
And warrants the creation
Of this fifth part of the Earth,
Which should seem an after-birth,
Not conceived in the Beginning
(For God blessed his work at first,
And saw that it was good),
But emerged at the first sinning,
When the ground was therefore cursed; –
And hence this barren wood!

Kangaroo, Kangaroo!
Tho' at first sight we should say,
In thy nature that there may
Contradiction be involved,
Yet, like discord well resolved,
It is quickly harmonized.
Sphynx or mermaid realized.
Or centaur unfabulous,
Would scarce be more prodigious,
Or Labyrinthine Minotaur,
With which great Theseus did war,
Or Pegasus poetical.
Or hippogriff – chimeras all!
But, what Nature would compile,
Nature knows to reconcile;
And Wisdom, ever at her side,
Of all his children's justified.

She had made the squirrel fragile;
She had made the bounding hart;

But a third so strong and agile
Was beyond ev'n Nature's art.
So she join'd the former two
    In thee, Kangaroo!

To describe thee, it is hard:
Converse of the camélopard,
Which beginneth camel-wise,
But endeth of the panther size,
Thy fore half, it would appear,
Had belonged to some 'small deer',
Such as liveth in a tree;
By thy hinder, thou should'st be
A large animal of chase,
Bounding o'er the forest's space; –
Joined by some divine mistake,
None but Nature's hand can make –
Nature, in her wisdom's play,
On Creation's holiday.

For howsoe'er anomalous,
Thou yet art not incongruous,
Repugnant or preposterous.
Better-proportioned animal,
More graceful or ethereal,
Was never followed by the hound,
With fifty steps to thy one bound.
Thou can'st not be amended: no;
Be as thou art; thou best art so.

When sooty swans are once more rare,
And duck-moles the Museum's care,
Be still the glory of this land,
Happiest Work of finest Hand!

BARRON FIELD 1786–1846

13 *An Enormous Puppy*

An enormous puppy was looking down at her with large round eyes, and feebly stretching out one paw, trying to touch her. 'Poor little thing!' said Alice, in a coaxing tone, and she tried hard to whistle to it; but she was terribly frightened all the time at the thought that it might be hungry, in which case it would be very likely to eat her up in spite of all her coaxing.

Hardly knowing what she did, she picked up a little bit of stick, and held it out to the puppy; whereupon the puppy jumped into the air off all its feet at once, with a yelp of delight, and rushed at the stick, and made believe to worry it; then Alice dodged behind a great thistle, to keep herself from being run over; and the moment she appeared on the other side, the puppy made another rush at the stick, and tumbled head over heels in its hurry to get hold of it; then Alice, thinking it was very like having a game of play with a cart-horse, and expecting every moment to be trampled under its feet, ran round the thistle again; then the puppy began a series of short charges at the stick, running a very little way forwards each time and a long way back, and barking hoarsely all the while, till at last it sat down a good way off, panting, with its tongue hanging out of its mouth, and its great eyes half shut.

LEWIS CARROLL 1832–1898 *Alice's Adventures in Wonderland*

14 *The Prettiest Mammal*

It would be hard in any company of men well acquainted with our fauna to find two persons to agree as to which is the handsomest or prettiest of our indigenous mammals.

'Undoubtedly the stag,' one would exclaim: another

would perhaps venture to name the field-mouse, or dor-mouse, or the water-vole, that quaint miniature beaver in his sealskin-coloured coat, sitting erect on the streamlet's margin busily nibbling at the pale end of a polished rush-stalk which he has cut off at the root and is now holding close to his breast with his little hands.

Anyone who had thus seen him, the brown sunlit bank, with its hanging drapery of foliage and flowers for back-ground, reflected in the clear water below, could well be pardoned for praising his beauty and giving him the palm.

W. H. HUDSON 1841–1922 Book of a Naturalist

15 A Poor Ass

'Twas by a poor ass, who had just turned in with a couple of large panniers upon his back, to collect eleemosynary turnip-tops and cabbage leaves, and stood dubious, with his two fore feet on the inside of the threshold, and with his two hinder feet towards the street, as not knowing very well whether he was to go in or no.

Now, 'tis an animal (be in what hurry I may) I cannot bear to strike; there is a patient endurance of sufferings wrote so unaffectedly in his looks and carriage, which pleads so mightily for him, that it always disarms me; and to that degree, that I do not like to speak unkindly to him: on the contrary, meet him where I will, whether in town or country, in cart or under panniers, – whether in liberty or bondage, I have ever something civil to say to him on my part; and, as one word begets another (if he has as little to do as I) I generally fall into conversation with him; and surely never is my imagination so busy as in framing his responses from the etchings of his countenance, – and where those carry me not deep enough, – in flying from my own heart into his, and seeing what is natural for an ass to think,

– as well as a man upon the occasion. In truth, it is the only creature of all the classes of beings below me, with whom I can do this; for parrots, jackdaws, etc., I never exchange a word with them – nor with apes, etc., for pretty near the same reason; they act by rote, as the others speak by it, and equally make me silent: nay, my dog and my cat though I value them both (and, for my dog, he would speak if he could) yet somehow or other, they neither of them possess the talents for conversation; I can make nothing of a discourse with them beyond the proposition, the reply, and rejoinder, which terminated my father's and my mother's conversations in his beds of justice; – and those uttered, there's an end of the dialogue.

LAURENCE STERNE 1713–1768 *Tristram Shandy*

16 *Aunt Patsy, Snakes and Bats*

Along the outside of the front fence ran the country road, dusty in the summertime and a good place for snakes – they liked to lie in it and sun themselves; when they were rattlesnakes or puff adders we killed them; when they were black snakes or racers or belonged to the fabled 'hoop' breed we fled without shame; when they were 'house snakes' or 'garters' we carried them home and put them in Aunt Patsy's work basket for a surprise; for she was prejudiced against snakes, and always when she took the basket in her lap and they began to climb out of it it disordered her mind. She never could seem to get used to them; her opportunities went for nothing. And she was always cold towards bats, too, and could not bear them; and yet I think a bat is as friendly a bird as there is. My mother was Aunt Patsy's sister and had the same wild superstitions. A bat is beautifully soft and silky; I do not know any creature that is pleasanter to the touch or is more graceful for caressings, if offered in the right spirit. I know all about these coleoptera because our great cave, three miles below Hannibal, was multitudinously stocked with them and often I brought them home to amuse my mother with. It was easy to manage if it was a school day because then I had ostensibly been to school and hadn't any bats. She was not a suspicious person but full of trust and confidence; and when I said, 'There's something in my coat pocket for you', she would put her hand in. But she always took it out again, herself; I didn't have to tell her. It was remarkable the way she couldn't learn to like private bats. The more experience she had the more she could not change her views.

MARK TWAIN 1835–1910 *The Autobiography of Mark Twain*

17 *Lines to a Dragon Fly*

Life (priest and poet say) is but a dream;
　　I wish no happier one than to be laid
　　Beneath some cool syringa's scented shade
Or wavy willow, by the running stream,
　　Brimful of Moral, where the Dragon Fly,
　　Wanders as careless and content as I.
Thanks for this fancy, insect king,
Of purple crest and filmy wing,
Who with indifference givest up
The water-lily's golden cup,
To come again and overlook
What I am writing in my book.
Believe me, most who read the line
Will read with hornier eyes than thine;
And yet their souls shall live for ever,
And thine drop dead into the river!
God pardon them, O insect king,
Who fancy so unjust a thing!

WALTER SAVAGE LANDOR 1775–1864

18 *Hunters and Hawkers*

Included among stupid delights is gambling – of which the Utopians have heard but never practised – and also hunting and hawking . . . Where is the pleasure in listening to the barking and howling of dogs? And why is there greater amusement in watching a dog chase a hare, than in watching one dog chase another? Both activities involve speed – if speed is what amuses you. But if you are attracted to the idea of being in at the kill, and seeing an animal being torn apart in front of you, you ought rather to be inspired to pity at the sight of a weak, timid, innocent little hare being devoured by a strong, fierce, cruel dog.

So Utopians consider hunting as unworthy of free men, and leave it to the butchers. They consider hunting to be the meanest part of the butchers' trade, compared to the other parts which are useful and honourable. A butcher kills an animal from necessity, whereas a hunter kills and mutilates for his own pleasure. They say that such a form of blood-lust is not even found amongst animals, unless they are savage by nature, or have been constantly used for this cruel sport.

Although such sports are generally regarded as pleasures, the Utopians are convinced that they have nothing to do with true pleasure, since there is nothing naturally enjoyable about them. The fact that many people do derive enjoyment from them, does not cause the people of Utopia to alter their opinion.

THOMAS MORE 1478–1535 *Utopia*

19 *Kitten Overboard*

A most tragical incident fell out this day at sea. While the ship was under sail, but making, as will appear, no great way, a kitten, one of four of the feline inhabitants of the cabin, fell from the window into the water: an alarm was immediately given to the Captain, who was then upon deck, and received it with the utmost concern. He immediately gave orders to the steersman in favour of the poor thing, as he called it; the sails were instantly slackened, and all hands, as the phrase is, employed to recover the poor animal. I was, I own, extremely surprised at all this; less, indeed, at the Captain's extreme tenderness, than at his conceiving any possibility of success; for, if puss had had nine thousand, instead of nine lives, I concluded they had been all lost. The boatswain, however, had more sanguine hopes; for, having stripped himself of his jacket, breeches, and shirt, he leapt boldly into the water, and, to my great astonishment, in a few minutes returned to the ship, bearing the motionless animal in his mouth. Nor was this, I observed, a matter of such great difficulty as it appeared to my ignorance, and possibly may seem to that of my fresh-water reader: the kitten was now exposed to air and sun on the deck, where its life, of which it retained no symptoms, was despaired of by all.

The Captain's humanity, if I may so call it, did not so totally destroy his philosophy, as to make him yield himself up to affliction on this melancholy occasion. Having felt his loss like a man, he resolved to show he could bear it like one; and, having declared, he had rather have lost a cask of rum or brandy, betook himself to threshing at backgammon with the *Portuguese* friar, in which innocent amusement they passed their leisure hours.

But as I have, perhaps, a little too wantonly endeavoured to raise the tender passions of my readers, in this narrative,

I should think myself unpardonable if I concluded it, without giving them the satisfaction of hearing that the kitten at last recovered, to the great joy of the good Captain.

HENRY FIELDING 1707–1754 *Journal of a Voyage to Lisbon*

20 *The Lake of Beauty*

Let your mind be quiet, realising the beauty of the world,
       and the immense the boundless treasures that it
       holds in store.
All that you have within you, all that your heart desires,
       all that your Nature so specially fits you for – that
       or the counterpart of it waits embedded in the great
       Whole, for you. It will surely come to you.
Yet equally surely not one moment before its appointed
       time will it come. All your crying and fever and
       reaching out of hands will make no difference.
Therefore do not begin that game at all.

Do not recklessly spill the waters of your mind in this
       direction and in that, lest you become like a spring
       lost and dissipated in the desert.
But draw them together into a little compass, and hold
       them still, so still;
And let them become clear, so clear – so limpid, so mirror-
       like;
At last the mountains and the sky shall glass themselves in
       peaceful beauty,
And the antelope shall descend to drink, and to gaze at his
       reflected image, and the lion to quench his thirst,
And Love himself shall come and bend over, and catch his
       own likeness in you.

EDWARD CARPENTER 1844–1929

Hymn: All Things Bright and Beautiful

All things bright and beautiful,
All creatures great and small,
All things wise and wonderful,
The Lord God made them all.

Each little flower that opens,
Each little bird that sings,
He made their glowing colours,
He made their tiny wings.

The purple-headed mountain,
The river running by,
The sunset and the morning,
That brightens up the sky.

The cold wind in the winter,
The pleasant summer sun,
The ripe fruits in the garden,
He made them every one.

The tall trees in the greenwood,
The meadows for our play,
The rushes by the water,
To gather every day.

He gave us eyes to see them,
And lips that we may tell
How great is God Almighty,
Who has made all things well.

C. F. ALEXANDER 1818–1895

9

LET US MAKE MAN
IN OUR IMAGE

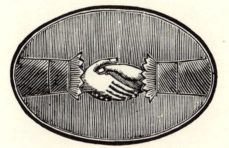

Be thou a light unto my eyes, music to mine ears, sweetness to my taste, and full contentment to my heart. Be thou my sunshine in the day, my food at table, my repose in the night, my clothing in nakedness, and my succour in all necessities. Lord Jesu, I give thee my body, my soul, my substance, my fame, my friends, my liberty and my life. Dispose of me and all that is mine as it may seem best to thee and to the glory of thy blessed name.

JOHN COSIN 1594–1672

The hand of the Lord was upon me, and carried me out in the spirit of the Lord, and set me down in the midst of the valley which was full of bones.

And he said unto me, Son of man, can these bones live? And I answered, O Lord God, thou knowest. And he said unto me, Prophesy upon these bones, and say unto them, O ye dry bones, hear the word of the Lord. Thus saith the Lord God unto these bones; Behold, I will cause breath to enter into you, and ye shall live: and I will lay sinews upon you, and will bring up flesh upon you, and cover you with skin, and put breath in you, and ye shall live; and ye shall know that I am the Lord. So I prophesied as I was commanded: and as I prophesied, there was a noise, and behold a shaking, and the bones came together, bone to his bone. And when I beheld, lo, the sinews and the flesh came up upon them, and the skin covered them above: but there was no breath in them.

Then said he unto me, Prophesy unto the wind, prophesy, son of man, and say to the wind, Thus saith the Lord God; Come from the four winds, O breath, and breathe upon these slain, that they may live. So I prophesied as he commanded me, and the breath came into them, and they lived, and stood up upon their feet, an exceeding great army.

EZEKIEL 37: 1, 4–10

If any man be in Christ, he is a new creature: old things are passed away; behold, all things are become new. And all things are of God, who hath reconciled us to himself by Jesus Christ, and hath given to us the ministry of reconciliation.

2 CORINTHIANS 5: 17–18

1 *In Unison with God*

The life of Adam, that is to say, the 'breath' which was to give actuality and existence and movement to the whole person of man, had mysteriously proceeded from the intimate depths of God's own life. Adam was created not merely as a living and moving animal who obeyed the command and will of God. He was created as a 'son' of God because his life shared something of the reality of God's own breath or Spirit. For 'breath' is the same as 'spirit.'

If the expression may be permitted, Adam's very existence was to be a kind of 'inspiration'. God intended not only to conserve and maintain Adam's bodily life. He would also foster and increase, even more directly and intimately, the spiritual life and activity which were the main reason for Adam's existence.

Adam, then, was meant from the very first to live and breathe in unison with God.

For him, then, to live would mean to 'be inspired' – to see things as God saw them, to love them as he loved them, to be moved in all things ecstatically by the Spirit of God.

THOMAS MERTON 1915–1968 *The New Man*

2 *Know Thyself*

Know then thyself, presume not God to scan;
The proper study of mankind is Man.
Placed on this isthmus of a middle state,
A being darkly wise and rudely great:
With too much knowledge for the Sceptic side,
With too much weakness for the Stoic's pride,
He hangs between; in doubt to act or rest,
In doubt to deem himself a God or Beast,

In doubt his mind or body to prefer;
Born but to die, and reasoning but to err;
Alike in ignorance, his reason such
Whether he thinks too little or too much:
Chaos of thought and passion, all confused;
Still by himself abused, or disabused;
Created half to rise and half to fall;
Great lord of all things, yet a prey to all;
Sole judge of truth, in endless error hurled:
The glory, jest, and riddle of the world!

ALEXANDER POPE 1688–1744

3 *Kinship with Nature*

No man or woman begins to live a full life until they realise they live in the presence of something greater, outside and beyond themselves. Self-consciousness truly means that you are standing over against that other than yourself and you cannot be living in truth. Wonder is at the base of true living, and wonder leads to worship and after that the great other than self; it is yet kin to you, you are one with it. Then you begin to live more completely and realise the kinship between you and Nature, that out of Nature you came and are part and parcel with it, this brings nearer faith, which is self-conscious life (opposed to birds, trees, etc.), reaching out to perfection.

G. A. STUDDERT-KENNEDY 1883–1929 *The New Man in Christ*

4 *United with Beauty*

We do not want merely to *see* beauty. We want something else which can hardly be put into words – to be united with the beauty we see, to pass into it, to receive it into ourselves, to bathe in it, to become part of it. That is why we have peopled air and earth and water with gods and goddesses and nymphs and elves – that, though we cannot, yet these projections can, enjoy themselves that beauty, grace and power of which Nature is the image. For if we take the imagery of Scripture seriously, if we believe that God will one day *give* us the morning star and cause us to *put on* the splendour of the sun, then we may surmise that both the ancient myths and the modern poetry, so false as history, may be very near the truth as prophecy. At present we are on the outside of the world, the wrong side of the door. We discern the freshness and purity of morning, but they do not make us fresh and pure. We cannot mingle with the splendours we see. But all the leaves of the New Testament are rustling with the rumour that it will not always be so. Someday, God willing, we shall get *in*. When human souls have become perfect in voluntary obedience as the inanimate creation is in its lifeless obedience, they will put on its glory, or, rather, that greater glory of which Nature is only the first sketch. We are summoned to pass in through Nature, beyond her, into that splendour which she fitfully reflects.

C. S. LEWIS 1898–1963 'The Weight of Glory'

5 *The World was Mine*

The corn was orient and immortal wheat, which never should be reaped, nor was ever sown. I thought it had stood from everlasting to everlasting. The dust and stones of the street were as precious as gold; the gates were at first the end of the world. The green trees, when I saw them first through one of the gates, transported and ravished me: their sweetness and unusual beauty made my heart to leap, and almost mad with ecstasy, they were such strange and wonderful things. The Men! O what venerable and reverend creatures did the aged seem! Immortal Cherubims! And young men glittering and sparkling Angels, and maids strange seraphic pieces of life and beauty! Boys and girls, tumbling in the street and playing, were moving jewels. I knew not that they were born or should die; but all things abided eternally as they were in their proper places. Eternity was manifest in the light of the day, and something infinite behind everything appeared, which talked with my expectation and moved my desire. The city seemed to stand in Eden, or to be built in Heaven. The streets were mine, the temple was mine, the people were mine, their clothes and gold and silver were mine, as much as their sparkling eyes, fair skins and ruddy faces. The skies were mine, and so were the sun and moon and stars; and all the World was mine, and I the only spectator and enjoyer of it. I knew no churlish proprieties nor bounds, nor divisions: but all proprieties and divisions were mine; all treasures and the possessors of them.

THOMAS TRAHERNE 1637–1674 *Centuries of Meditations*

6 *The Worship of Nature*

The harp at Nature's advent strung
    Has never ceased to play;
The song the stars of morning sung
    Has never died away.

And prayer is made, and praise is given,
    By all things near and far;
The ocean looketh up to heaven,
    And mirrors every star.

Its waves are kneeling on the strand,
    As kneels the human knee,
Their white locks bowing to the sand,
    The priesthood of the sea!

They pour their glittering treasures forth,
    Their gifts of pearl they bring,
And all the listening hills of earth
    Take up the song they sing.

The green earth sends her incense up
    From many a mountain shrine;
From folded leaf and dewy cup
    She pours her sacred wine.

The mists above the morning rills
    Rise white as wings of prayer;
The altar-curtains of the hills
    Are sunset's purple air.

The winds with hymns of praise are loud,
    Or low with sobs of pain, –
The thunder-organ of the cloud,
    The dropping tears of rain.

With drooping head and branches crossed
    The twilight forest grieves,
Or speaks with tongues of Pentecost
    From all its sunlit leaves.

The blue sky is the temple's arch,
    Its transept earth and air,
The music of its starry march
    The chorus of a prayer.

So Nature keeps the reverent frame
    With which her years began,
And all her signs and voices shame
    The prayerless heart of man.

JOHN GREENLEAF WHITTIER 1807–1892

7 *Taking Delight*

Among the mind's powers is one that comes of itself to many children and artists. It need not be lost, to the end of his days, by anyone who has ever had it. This is the power of taking delight in a thing, or rather in anything, everything, not as a means to some other end, but just because it is what it is, as the lover dotes on whatever may be the traits of the beloved object. A child in the full health of his mind will put his hand flat on the summer turf, feel it, and give a little shiver of private glee at the elastic firmness of the globe. He is not thinking how well it will do for some game or to feed sheep upon. That would be the way of the wooer whose mind runs on his mistress's money. The child's is sheer affection, the true ecstatic sense of the thing's inherent characteristics. No matter what the things may be, no matter what they are good or no good for, there they are, each with a thrilling unique look and feel of its own, like a face; the iron astringently cool under its paint, the painted wood familiarly warmer, the clod crumbling enchantingly down in the hands, with its little dry smell of the sun and of hot nettles; each common thing a personality marked by delicious differences.

This joy of an Adam new to the garden and just looking round is brought by the normal child to the things that he does as well as those that he sees. To be suffered to do some plain work with the real spade used by mankind can give him a mystical exaltation: to come home with his legs, as the French say, re-entering his body from the fatigue of helping the gardener to weed beds sends him to sleep in the glow of a beatitude that is an end in itself . . .

The right education, if we could find it, would work up this creative faculty of delight into all its branching possibilities of knowledge, wisdom, and nobility. Of all three it is the beginning, condition, or raw material.

C. E. MONTAGUE 1867–1928 *Disenchantment*

8 *There is a Pleasure*

There is a pleasure in the pathless woods,
There is a rapture on the lonely shore,
There is society, where none intrudes,
By the deep Sea, and music in its roar:
I love not Man the less, but Nature more,
From these our interviews, in which I steal
From all I may be, or have been before,
To mingle with the Universe, and feel
What I can ne'er express, yet can not all conceal.

GEORGE BYRON 1788–1824 'Childe Harold's Pilgrimage'

9 *Content with the Universe*

He shall know the celandine, and the frigid, sightless flowers
of the woods, spurge and spurge laurel, dogs' mercury,
wood-sorrel and queer four-leaved herb-paris fit to trim a
bonnet with its purple dot. He shall see the marshes gold
with flags and kingcups and find shepherd's purse on a slag-
heap. He shall know the tree-flowers, scented lime-tassels,
blood-pink, larch-tufts, white strands of the Spanish chestnut
and tattered oak-plumes. He shall know orchids, mauve-
winged bees and claret-coloured flies climbing up from mot-
tled leaves. He shall see June red and white with ragged
robin and cow parsley and the two campions. He shall tell
a dandelion from sow thistle or goat's beard. He shall know
the field flowers, lady's bed-straw and lady's slipper, purple
mallow, blue chicory and the cranesbills – dusky, bloody
and blue as heaven. In the cool summer wind he shall listen
to the rattle of harebells against the whistle of a distant train,
shall watch clover brush and scabious nod, pinch the ample
vetches, and savour the virgin turf. He shall know grasses,

timothy and wag-wanton, and dust his finger-tips in York-
shire fog. By the river he shall know pink willow-herb and
purple spikes of loosestrife, and the sweetshop smell of
water-mint where the rat dives silently from its hole. He
shall know the velvet leaves and yellow spike of the old
dowager, mullein, recognize the whole company of thistles,
and greet the relatives of the nettle, wound-wort and hore-
hound, yellow rattle, betony, bugle and archangel. In
autumn, he shall know the hedge lanterns, hips and haws
and bryony. At Christmas he shall climb an old apple-tree
for mistletoe, and know whom to kiss and how.

He shall know the butterflies that suck the brambles,
common whites and marbled white, orange-tip, brimstone,
and the carnivorous clouded yellows. He shall watch fritillar-
ies, pearl-bordered and silver-washed, flit like fireballs across
the sunlit rides. He shall see that family of capitalists, peacock, painted lady, red admiral and the tortoiseshells, uncurl
their trunks to suck blood from bruised plums, while the
purple emperor and white admiral glut themselves on the
bowels of a rabbit. He shall know the jagged comma, printed
with a white c, the manx-tailed iridescent hair-streaks, and
the skippers demure as charwomen on Monday morning.
He shall run to the glint of silver on a chalk-hill blue – glint
of a breeze on water beneath an open sky – and shall follow
the brown explorers, meadow, brown argus, speckled wood
and ringlet. He shall see death and revolution in the burnet
moth, black and red, crawling from a house of yellow talc
tied half-way up a tall grass. He shall know more rational
moths, who like the night, the gaudy tigers, cream-spot and
scarlet, and the red and yellow under-wings. He shall hear
the humming-bird hawk moth arrive like an air-raid on the
garden at dusk, and know the other hawks, pink sleek-
bodied elephant, poplar, lime, and death's head. He shall
count the pinions of the plume moths, and find the large
emerald waiting in the rain-dewed grass.

All these I learnt when I was a child and each recalls a

place or occasion that might otherwise be lost. They were my own discoveries. They taught me to look at the world with my own eyes and with attention. They gave me a first content with the universe. Town-dwellers lack this intimate content, but my son shall have it.

ROBERT BYRON 1905–1941 *Little Innocents*

10 *Eppie's Little World*

Eppie was a creature of endless claims and ever-growing desires, seeking and loving sunshine, and living sounds, and living movements; making trial of everything, with trust in new joy, and stirring the human kindness in all eyes that looked on her. The gold had kept his thoughts in an ever-repeated circle, leading to nothing beyond itself; but Eppie was an object compacted of changes and hopes that forced his thoughts onward, and carried them far away from their old eager pacing towards the same blank limit – carried them away to the new things that would come with the coming years, when Eppie would have learned to understand how her father Silas cared for her; and made him look for images of that time in the ties and charities that bound together the families of his neighbours. The gold had asked that he should sit weaving longer and longer, deafened and blinded more and more to all things except the monotony of his loom and the repetition of his web; but Eppie called him away from his weaving, and made him think all its pauses a holiday, re-awakening his senses with her fresh life, even to the old winter-flies that came crawling forth in the early spring sunshine, and warming him into joy because *she* had joy.

And when the sunshine grew strong and lasting, so that the buttercups were thick in the meadows, Silas might be seen in the sunny mid-day, or in the late afternoon when the shadows were lengthening under the hedgerows, strolling out with uncovered head to carry Eppie beyond the Stone-pits to where the flowers grew, till they reached some favourite bank where he could sit down, while Eppie toddled to pluck the flowers, and make remarks to the winged things that murmured happily above the bright petals, calling 'Dad-dad's' attention continually by bringing him the flowers. Then she would turn her ear to some sudden bird-note, and Silas learned to please her by making signs of hushed still-ness, that they might listen for the note to come again: so that when it came, she set up her small back and laughed with gurgling triumph. Sitting on the banks in this way, Silas began to look for the once familiar herbs again; and as the leaves, with their unchanged outline and markings, lay on his palm, there was a sense of crowding remembrances from which he turned away timidly, taking refuge in Eppie's little world, that lay lightly on his enfeebled spirit.

GEORGE ELIOT 1819–1880 *Silas Marner*

11 *Loving the Country*

You can love the country in two quite different ways, as a cat loves it and as a dog loves it. My mother was like a cat. She responded to the beauty, the peace and the solitude that it offered. She found this in her garden and she found it too in the countryside beyond. Solitude. She was happiest alone. Once, when she was going for a walk, I asked if I could come with her. 'No,' she said, 'but come and meet me on my way back. I like best being met.' And so we spent a lot of time meeting her. She would walk to the village and half an hour later my father and I would set off up the hill and hope that somewhere before we reached the top we would see her coming round the corner. Or it might be the other way round, and she would meet us as we drove home (choosing the pretty way, of course) after spending the morning playing golf. At night, before going to bed, she would walk up to the forest, two miles along the road, until she was level with Gill's Lap. On these occasions I sometimes accompanied her. It was different in the dark. You could be with someone and they would be there if you felt you wanted them, and if you didn't you could forget them. Now and again, on our way, a car would come by: blinding lights, a roar and a whoosh of wind that seemed to suck you out into the road in their wake. We clung to each other, standing against the hedge, until they were gone. Then on again. We both loved the country at night, the black shapes of the trees, the tiny spots of light from wayside cottages, the sound of the wind bustling about its invisible business. We scarcely talked, absorbed in our private thoughts.

If my mother was a cat, my father was surely a dog. He was a Londoner, a real Londoner with a deep love of London in his bones. For him the country had always been, not where you lived, but where you went. Where you went on holiday. Where you went to do something – to ride a bicycle, to climb a hill, to look for birds' nests, to play golf. Like a dog, he couldn't just *be* in the country, sitting or strolling aimlessly. It had to be a proper walk, a walk with a purpose, planned beforehand, worked out on the map even. And you couldn't go alone; you had to be with somebody, with me perhaps, or with the whole family, Nanny included. Like a dog, too, he was happiest of all when chasing a ball.

CHRISTOPHER MILNE *b.* 1920 *The Enchanted Places*

12 *The Elements*

Man is permitted much
    To scan and learn
    In Nature's frame;
Till he well-nigh can tame
Brute mischiefs and can touch
Invisible things, and turn
All warring ills to purposes of good.
    Thus, as a god below,
    He can control,
And harmonise, what seems amiss to flow
    As severed from the whole
    And dimly understood.

But o'er the elements
    One Hand alone
    One Hand has sway.
What influence day by day
In straiter belt prevents
The impious Ocean, thrown
Alternate o'er the ever-sounding shore?
    Or who has eye to trace
    How the Plague came?
Forerun the doublings of the Tempest's race?
    Or the Air's weight and flame
    On a set scale explore?

    Thus God has willed
That man, when fully skilled,
Still gropes in twilight dim;
Encompassed all his hours
    By fearfullest powers
    Inflexible to him.
That so he may discern
    His feebleness,

And e'en for earth's success
To Him in wisdom turn,
Who holds for us the keys of either home,
Earth and the world to come.

JOHN HENRY NEWMAN 1801–1890

13 *Delusion*

Man thinks of himself as a creator instead of a user, and this delusion is robbing him, not only of his natural heritage, but perhaps of his future.

HELEN HOOVER *b.* 1935 *The Long-Shadowed Forest*

14 *Sweet and Honest Talk*

The more I get to know of the agricultural labourers, the better I like them. As I listen to their simple, often coarse, but somehow sweet and honest talk, so shrewd withal, I get a glimpse of the roots of humanity, sharing with the earth its endurance and soundness of heart, and among themselves a warmth and fair dealing very different from the world of towns. The primitive still resides in these men, changeless for seven thousand years, and through them we can see the true nature of man before he went to war and followed crazy ideas and built temples and set up priests and kings and, after them, financiers. Simple souls enough. If you have an accident on the road, there would not be one of them who would not stop and say, 'Eh, zur, you be in the ditch', but hardly one of them who would not forgo his work and victuals to help you out and entreat you kindly.

H. J. MASSINGHAM 1888–1952 *Wold Without End*

15 *The First Duty of Man*

For man to live fully it is necessary for him, as for every other organism, to be adapted to his surroundings; but man can do so on a new level, denied to other organisms, in the world of mind. His life, if it is to be the best life possible, must be seen, felt and practically lived in its relation to the rest of the universe. If he fails to take account of any essential of reality, or if he misinterprets it, woe to him: the omission or the mistake will bring its retribution.

To this task of relating his life to the rest of reality he must bring all his powers; but the mortar which must hold all together if the construction is to hold is the spirit of love and reverence. Such a construction so held together is a true and developed religion.

That is what orthodox theism means when it says that the knowledge and love of God is the first duty of man.

JULIAN HUXLEY 1887–1975 *Religion Without Revelation*

16 *Sweet Smiling Village*

Sweet smiling village, loveliest of the lawn,
Thy sports are fled, and all thy charms withdrawn;
Amidst thy bowers the tyrant's hand is seen,
And desolation saddens all thy green:
One only master grasps the whole domain,
And half a tillage stints thy smiling plain;
No more thy glassy brook reflects the day,
But, choked with sedges, works its weedy way;
Among thy glades, a solitary guest,
The hollow-sounding bittern guards its nest;
Amidst thy desert walks the lapwing flies,
And tires their echoes with unvaried cries.

Sunk are thy bowers, in shapeless ruin all,
And the long grass o'ertops the mouldering wall;
And trembling, shrinking from the spoiler's hand,
Far, far away thy children leave the land.

Ill fares the land, to hastening ills a prey,
Where wealth accumulates, and men decay:
Princes and lords may flourish, or may fade;
A breath can make them, as a breath has made;
But a bold peasantry, their country's pride,
When once destroyed, can never be supplied.

OLIVER GOLDSMITH *c.* 1730–1774 'The Deserted Village'

17 *Art in its Perfection*

The highest beauty of form must be taken from nature; but
it is an art of long deduction and great experience to know
how to find it.

We must not content ourselves with merely admiring and
relishing; we must enter into the principles on which the
work is wrought: these do not swim on the superficies, and
consequently are not open to superficial observers.

Art in its perfection is not ostentatious; it lies hid and
works its effect, itself unseen. It is the proper study
and labour of an artist to uncover and find out the latent cause
of conspicuous beauties, and from thence form principles for
his own conduct; such an examination is a continual exertion
of the mind; as great, perhaps, as that of the Artist whose
works he is thus studying.

JOSHUA REYNOLDS 1723–1792 *Sixth Discourse*

18 *Glorious Harmony*

Nature contains the elements, in colour and form, of all pictures, as the keyboard contains the notes of all music.

But the artist is born to pick, and choose, and group with science, these elements, that the result may be beautiful – as the musician gathers his notes, and forms his chords, until he bring forth from chaos glorious harmony.

To say to the painter, that Nature is to be taken as she is, is to say to the player, that he may sit on the piano . . .

To him her secrets are unfolded, to him her lessons have become gradually clear. He looks at her flower, not with the enlarging lens, that he may gather facts for the botanist, but with the light of the one who sees in her choice selection of brilliant tones and delicate tints, suggestions of future harmonies.

He does not confine himself to purposeless copying, without thought, each blade of grass, as commended by the inconsequent, but, in the long curve of the narrow leaf, corrected by the straight tall stem, he learns how grace is wedded to dignity, how strength enhances sweetness, that elegance shall be the result.

In the citron wing of the pale butterfly, with its dainty spots of orange, he sees before him the stately halls of fair gold, with their slender saffron pillars, and is taught how the delicate drawing high upon the walls shall be traced in tender tones of orpiment, and repeated by the base in notes of graver hue.

In all that is dainty and lovable he finds hints for his own combinations, and *thus* is Nature ever his resource and always at his service, and to him is naught refused.

JAMES ABBOTT MCNEILL WHISTLER 1834–1903
The Gentle Art of Making Enemies

19 *Preserver of Creation*

God loves a cheerful giver, for God gives cheerfully and freely and liberally. 'He that gives to the poor, lends to the Lord, for the Lord restores him double again' (Prov. 19:17). But people's hearts are hardened, and they mind not to disgrace the truth; and the custom of the cries of the blind, the lame, the widows, and the fatherless have taken away the sense of compassion. Therefore, let there be a storehouse where all may be relieved, and let none want, that all may have enough. The Lord can take away from you as much in a week that would (it may be) serve thousands of the poor, and cross you by sea and by land for your hardheartedness; which otherwise you would see as a blessing and feel as a blessing both within and without, in store, in field, by sea and land.

As you come into the wisdom of God, and stand in it, and are preservers of the creation, then God will bless you, and what you take in hand will prosper. A preserver of the creation visits the sick and the fatherless, and causes not the blind to wander. Cannot God bring the proudest of you all down, and make you as poor as them that wander in the streets, because you do not do good in your lifetime? Therefore, come to work, and do the work of the Lord while you have poor, you great ones; and come to the feeling of these things, you magistrates, that none of these may lie up and down your streets, while it is in your power to do good.

GEORGE FOX 1624–1691
Letter to All the Magistrates in London

20 *Praising the Creator*

What is more useful, what is more healthful, than to recollect the immeasurable kindnesses of your Creator in sweet meditation? Consider how in the very beginning of his creation he conferred a great excellence and dignity upon you, and weigh well with what love and reverence he is to be worshipped. In creating the universe of things visible and invisible he ordained that human nature in its dignity should be more highly honoured than all the other creatures in the world.

See then the height of your creation, and consider the debt of love you owe in return. 'Let us make man,' said God, 'after our image and likeness.' If these words do not arouse you, if you are not entirely set on fire with love towards him, if you are not kindled into longing for him, what shall I say? Shall I think you are asleep? Shall I not rather think you are dead? . . .

You were created then to praise your Creator, so that wholly given up to his praises you might become ever more and more one with him, and hereafter might live happily. For the singing of his praise brings both justification here, and bliss hereafter.

ANSELM *c.* 1033–1109 'Meditation on the Dignity of Man'

Hymn: All People that on Earth do Dwell

All people that on earth do dwell,
Sing to the Lord with cheerful voice;
Him serve with fear, his praise forth tell,
Come ye before him and rejoice.

The Lord, ye know, is God indeed,
Without our aid he did us make;

We are his folk, he doth us feed
And for his sheep he doth us take.

O enter then his gates with praise,
Approach with joy his courts unto;
Praise, laud, and bless his name always,
For it is seemly so to do.

For why? the Lord our God is good:
His mercy is for ever sure;
His truth at all times firmly stood,
And shall from age to age endure.

To Father, Son and Holy Ghost,
The God whom heaven and earth adore,
From men and from the angel-host
Be praise and glory evermore.

WILLIAM KETHE *d. c.* 1599

10

AND GOD SAW THAT
IT WAS GOOD

Giver of all good things, we thank thee: for health and vigour; for the air that gives the breath of life, the sun that warms us, and the good food that makes us strong; for happy homes and for the friends we love; for all that makes it good to live. Make us thankful and eager to repay, by cheerfulness and kindliness, and by a readiness to help others. Freely we have received; let us freely give, in the name of him who gave his life for us, Jesus Christ our Lord.

THOMAS KEN 1637–1711

Praise ye the Lord. Praise ye the Lord from the heavens: praise him in the heights. Praise ye him, all his angels: praise ye him, all his hosts. Praise ye him, sun and moon: praise him, all ye stars of light. Praise him, ye heavens of heavens, and ye waters that be above the heavens. Let them praise the name of the Lord: for he commanded, and they were created. He hath also stablished them for ever and ever: he hath made a decree which shall not pass.

Praise the Lord from the earth, ye dragons, and all deeps: fire, and hail; snow, and vapours; stormy wind fulfilling his word: mountains, and all hills; fruitful trees, and all cedars: beasts, and all cattle; creeping things, and flying fowl: kings of the earth, and all people; princes, and all judges of the earth: both young men, and maidens; old men, and children: let them praise the name of the Lord: for his name alone is excellent; his glory is above the earth and heaven.

PSALM 148: 1–13

And he that sat upon the throne said, Behold, I make all things new. And he said unto me, Write: for these words are true and faithful. And he said unto me, It is done. I am Alpha and Omega, the beginning and the end. I will give unto him that is athirst of the fountain of the water of life freely. He that overcometh shall inherit all things; and I will be his God, and he shall be my son.

REVELATION 21: 5–7

1 *Seventh Day*

Passive I lie, looking up through leaves,
An eye only, one of the eyes of earth
That open at a myriad points at the living surface.
Eyes that earth opens see and delight
Because of the leaves, because of the unfolding of the leaves.
The folding, veining, imbrication, fluttering, resting,
The green and deepening manifold of the leaves.

Eyes of the earth know only delight
Untroubled by anything that I am, and I am nothing:
All that nature is, receive and recognize,
Pleased with the sky, the falling water and the flowers,
With bird and fish and the striations of stone.
Every natural form, living and moving
Delights these eyes that are no longer mine
That open upon earth and sky pure vision.
Nature sees, sees itself, is both seer and seen.

This is the divine repose, that watches
The ever-changing light and shadow, rock and sky and
        ocean.

KATHLEEN RAINE *b.* 1908

2 *God is Glorified*

God is glorified in the sun and moon, in the rare fabric of
the honeycombs, in the discipline of bees, in the economy
of pismires, in the little houses of birds, in the curiosity of
an eye, God being pleased to delight in those little images
and reflexes of himself from those pretty mirrors, which like
a crevice in a wall through a narrow perspective transmit the
species of a vast excellency.

JEREMY TAYLOR 1613–1667 *Twenty-eight Sermons*

3 *God's Grandeur*

The world is charged with the grandeur of God,
   It will flame out, like shining from shook foil;
   It gathers to a greatness, like the ooze of oil
Crushed. Why do men then now not reck his rod?
Generations have trod, have trod, have trod;
   And all is seared with trade; bleared, smeared with toil;
   And wears man's smudge and shares man's smell: the
      soil
Is bare now, nor can foot feel, being shod.

And for all this, nature is never spent;
   There lives the dearest freshness deep down things;
And though the last lights off the black West went
   Oh, morning, at the brown brink eastward, springs –
Because the Holy Ghost over the bent
   World broods with warm breast and with ah! bright
      wings.

               GERARD MANLEY HOPKINS 1844–1889

4 *Creation Restored*

While 'the whole creation groaneth together,' (whether men
attend or not,) their groans are not dispersed in idle air, but
enter into the ears of Him that made them. While his creatures 'travail together in pain,' he knoweth all their pain,
and is bringing them nearer and nearer to the birth, which
shall be accomplished in its season. He seeth 'the earnest
expectation' wherewith the whole animated creation 'waiteth
for' that final 'manifestation of the sons of God;' in which
'they themselves also shall be delivered' (not by annihilation;
annihilation is not deliverance) 'from the' present 'bondage

of corruption, into' a measure of 'the glorious liberty of the children of God.'

Nothing can be more express: away with vulgar prejudices, and let the plain word of God take place. They 'shall be delivered from the bondage of corruption into glorious liberty,' – even a measure, according as they are capable, of 'the liberty of the children of God' . . .

To descend to a few particulars: the whole brute creation will then, undoubtedly, be restored, not only to the vigour, strength, and swiftness which they had at their creation, but to a far higher degree of each than they ever enjoyed. They will be restored, not only to that measure of understanding which they had in paradise, but to a degree of it as much higher than that, as the understanding of an elephant is beyond that of a worm. And whatever affections they had in the garden of God, will be restored with vast increase; being exalted and refined in a manner which we ourselves are not now able to comprehend. The liberty they then had will be completely restored, and they will be free in all their motions. They will be delivered from all irregular appetites, from all unruly passions, from every disposition that is either evil in itself, or has any tendency to evil. No rage will be found in any creature, no fierceness, no cruelty, or thirst for blood. So far from it, that 'the wolf shall dwell with the lamb, the leopard shall lie down with the kid; the calf and the young lion together; and a little child shall lead them. The cow and the bear shall feed together; and the lion shall eat straw like the ox. They shall not hurt nor destroy in all my holy mountain.' (Isaiah 11:6 etc.)

JOHN WESLEY 1703–1791 *Sermons on Several Occasions*

5 *Love is the Great Hinge*

Love is the great Hinge upon which universal Nature turns.
The Creation is a transcript of the divine Goodness; and
every leaf in the Book of Nature reads us a lecture on the
wisdom and benevolence of its great Author. The Philos-
opher, inured to study and contemplation, untainted with
pride, and unbiased by prejudice, sees and acknowledges this
truth as incontestable, that the Supreme Being is wise, and
just, and good, and merciful . . . I shall therefore take it for
granted, that as God is wise and good, all his works and
appointments must be the effects of wisdom and goodness.

Upon this principle, every creature of God is good in its
kind; that is, it is such as it ought to be. For to suppose
otherwise, is to arraign the divine Wisdom for making it
such as it is. And as every creature is good in its kind, and
did not make itself what it is, but is such as it is solely by
the will and appointment of God, – it follows, that whatever
its perfections or defects may be, they cannot be owing to
any merit or demerit in the creature itself, being, not prior,
but consequential to its creation. There is not therefore in
nature any foundation for pride on account of perfection,
nor for contempt on account of defect.

HUMPRHY PRIMATT (18th century)
The Duty of Mercy and the Sin of Cruelty to Brute Animals

6 *Reconciliation*

Looking back on my own experiences they all converge
towards a kind of insight to which I cannot help ascribing
some metaphysical significance. The keynote of it is
invariably a reconciliation. It is as if the opposites of the
world, whose contradictoriness and conflict make all our

difficulties and troubles, were melted into unity. Not only do they, as contrasted species, belong to one and the same genus, but *one of the species*, the nobler and better one, *is itself the genus, and so soaks up and absorbs its opposite into itself.* This is a dark saying, I know, when thus expressed in terms of common logic, but I cannot wholly escape from its authority.

WILLIAM JAMES 1842–1910 *Varieties of Religious Experience*

7 *A Pastoral Hymn*

Happy choristers of air,
Who by your nimble flight draw near
　　His throne, whose wondrous story
　　And unconfinèd glory
Your notes still carol, whom your sound
And whom your plumy pipes rebound.

Yet do the lazy snails no less
The greatness of our Lord confess,
　　And those whom weight hath chained
　　And to the earth restrained,
Their ruder voices do as well,
Yea and the speechless fishes tell.

Great Lord, from whom each tree receives
Then pays again as rent, his leaves,
　　Thou dost in purple set
　　The rose and violet,
And giv'st the sickly lily white,
Yet in them all, the name doth write.

JOHN HALL 1627–1656

8 *And Now the Trembling Light*

And now the trembling light
Glimmers behind the little hills, and corn,
Ling'ring as loth to part: yet part thou must
And though than open day far pleasing more
(Ere yet the fields and pearlèd cups of flowers
    Twinkle in the parting light;)
Thee night shall hide, sweet visionary gleam
That softly lookest through the rising dew:
    Till all like silver bright
    The faithful Witness, pure, and white,
Shall look o'er yonder grassy hill,
At this village, safe, and still.

All is safe, and all is still,
Save what noise the watch-dog makes
Or the shrill cock the silence breaks
    Now and then.
    And now and then
    Hark! – once again
    The wether's bell
    To us doth tell
Some little stirring in the fold.

    Methinks the ling'ring, dying ray
    Of twilight time doth seem more fair,
And lights the soul up more than day,
    When widespread, sultry sunshines are.
Yet all is right, and all most fair;
For Thou, dear God, hast formèd all;
Thou deckest ev'ry little flower,
Thou girdest ev'ry planet ball
    And mark'st when sparrows fall.
Thou pourest out the golden day
    On corn-fields rip'ning in the sun

Up the side of some great hill
Ere the sickle has begun.

SAMUEL PALMER 1805–1881

9 *Pleasure it is*

Pleasure it is
To hear, I wis,
  The birdes sing.
The deer in the dale,
The sheep in the vale,
  The corn springing.

God's purveyance
For sustenance
  It is for man.
Then we always
To give him praise,
  And thank him then.

WILLIAM CORNISH d. 1523

10 *A Very Pretty Place*

My dear Robert,
   One passage in your letter a little displeased me. The rest
was nothing but kindness, which Robert's letters are ever
brimful of. You say that 'this world to you seems drained
of all its sweets!' At first I had hoped you only meant to
insinuate the high price of sugar! but I am afraid you meant
more. O Robert, I don't know what you call sweet. Honey
and the honeycomb, roses and violets, are yet in the earth.
The sun and moon yet reign in Heaven, and the lesser lights

keep up their pretty twinklings. Meats and drinks, sweet sights and sweet smells, a country walk, spring and autumn, follies and repentance, quarrels and reconcilements, have all a sweetness by turns. Good humour and good nature, friends at home that love you, and friends abroad that miss you, you possess all these things, and more innumerable, and these are all sweet things. You may extract honey from everything; do not go a-gathering after gall. The bees are wiser in their generation than the race of sonnet writers and complainers, Bowles's and Charlotte Smiths, and all that tribe, who can see no joys but what are past, and fill people's heads with notions of the unsatisfying nature of earthly comforts. I assure you I find this world a very pretty place.

CHARLES LAMB 1775–1834 Letter to Robert Lloyd

11 *A Thing of Beauty*

A thing of beauty is a joy for ever:
Its loveliness increases; it will never
Pass into nothingness; but still will keep
A bower quiet for us, and a sleep
Full of sweet dreams, and health, and quiet breathing.
Therefore, on every morrow, are we wreathing
A flowery band to bind us to the earth,
Spite of despondence, of the inhuman dearth
Of noble natures, of the gloomy days,
Of all the unhealthy and o'er-darkened ways
Made for our searching: yes, in spite of all,
Some shape of beauty moves away the pall
From our dark spirits. Such the sun, the moon,
Trees old, and young, sprouting a shady boon
For simple sheep; and such are daffodils
With the green world they live in; and clear rills
That for themselves a cooling covert make

'Gainst the hot season; the mid forest brake,
Rich with a sprinkling of fair musk-rose blooms:
And such too is the grandeur of the dooms
We have imagined for the mighty dead;
All lovely tales that we have heard or read:
An endless fountain of immortal drink,
Pouring unto us from the heaven's brink.
　　Nor do we merely feel these essences
For one short hour; no, even as the trees
That whisper round a temple become soon
Dear as the temple's self, so does the moon,
The passion poesy, glories infinite,
Haunt us till they become a cheering light
Unto our souls, and bound to us so fast,
That, whether there be shine, or gloom o'ercast,
They always must be with us, or we die.

JOHN KEATS 1795–1821 'Endymion'

12 *What a Beautiful Thing*

A very cold morning – hail and snow showers all day. We went to Brothers wood, intending to get plants, and to go along the shore of the lake to the foot. We did go a part of the way, but there was no pleasure in stepping along that difficult sauntering road in this ungenial weather. We turned again, and walked backwards and forwards in Brothers wood. William tired himself with seeking an epithet for the cuckoo. I sat a while upon my last summer seat, the mossy stone. William's, unoccupied, beside me, and the space between, where Coleridge has so often lain. The oak trees are just putting forth yellow knots of leaves. The ashes with their flowers passing away, and leaves coming out; the blue hyacinth is not quite full blown; gowans are coming out; marsh marigolds in full glory; the little star plant, a star without a flower. We took home a great load of gowans, and planted them about the orchard. After dinner I worked bread, then came and mended stockings beside William; he fell asleep. After tea I walked to Rydale for letters. It was a strange night. The hills were covered over with a slight covering of hail or snow, just so as to give them a hoary winter look with the black rocks. The woods looked miserable, the coppices green as grass, which looked quite unnatural, and they seemed half shrivelled up, as if they shrank from the air. O, thought I! what a beautiful thing God has made winter to be, by stripping the trees, and letting us see their shapes and forms. What a freedom does it seem to give to the storms!

DOROTHY WORDSWORTH 1771–1855 *Journals*

13 *A Riot of Forms and Colours*

When out of the riot of forms and colours in nature the artificer is able to co-ordinate the elements of a more comprehensible design, then it is that for brief moments he reaches harmony with the universal spirit. Sometimes in those seconds of insight time stands still, events past, present and future remain stationary like resting cattle spotted on the surface of a field, and the artist sees them as God sees time.

ROBERT GIBBINGS 1889–1958 *Sermons by Artists*

14 *Beauty, Goodness and Truth*

The Beauty of the world, as many have felt, is the strongest evidence we have of the goodness and benevolence of the Creator. Not, of course, that the world was made beautiful for our sakes. It is beautiful because its Author is beautiful;

and we should remember that when the old writers spoke of God as the Author of nature, they used the word in much the same sense as if we said that a man was the author of his own photograph. But we are allowed to see and enjoy beauty, although the gift cannot be proved to promote our own survival. It looks like a free gift of God. Beauty is a general quality of nature, and not only of organic nature; crystals are very beautiful. As in the case of the other ultimate values, the emotion of beauty is aroused by the meeting of mind and its object; and not only must the object be beautiful; the perceiving mind must also be beautiful and healthy. The vile or vulgar mind not only cannot discern beauty; it is a great destroyer of beauty everywhere.

The love of beauty is super-personal and disinterested, like all the spiritual values; it promotes common enjoyment and social sympathy. Unquestionably it is one of the three ultimate values, ranking with Goodness and Truth.

WILLIAM RALPH INGE 1860–1954 *Outspoken Essays*

15 *Transfiguration of Nature*

The Christian hope of the future is that this, the true meaning and message of the Incarnation, will come to be more deeply understood: and the demand on man's worshipping love and total self-offering, will receive a more complete response – a response stretching upward in awestruck contemplation to share that adoring vision of the Principle which is 'the inheritance of the saints in light,' and downwards and outwards in loving action, to embrace and so transform the whole world. When this happens, Christian sacramental worship will at last disclose its full meaning, and enter into its full heritage. For it will be recognized as the ritual sign of our deepest relation with Reality, and so of the mysterious splendour of our situation and our call: the successive life of man freely offered in oblation, and the abiding life of God in Christ received, not for our own sakes, but in order to achieve that transfiguration of the whole created universe, that shining forth of the splendour of the Holy, in which the aim of worship shall be fulfilled.

EVELYN UNDERHILL 1875–1941 *Worship*

16 *Thank Him for the Pleasures*

I will thank him for the pleasures given me through my senses, for the glory of the thunder, for the mystery of music, the singing of the birds and the laughter of children. I will thank him for the pleasures of seeing, for the delights through colour, for the awe of the sunset, the beauty of flowers, the smile of friendship and the look of love; for the changing beauty of the clouds, for the wild roses in the hedges, for the form and the beauty of birds, for the leaves on the trees in spring and autumn, for the witness of the leafless trees through the winter, teaching us that death is sleep and not destruction, for the sweetness of flowers and the scent of hay. Truly, O Lord, the earth is full of thy riches!

And yet, how much more I will thank and praise God for the strength of my body enabling me to work, for the refreshment of sleep, for my daily bread, for the days of painless health, for the gift of my mind and the gift of my conscience, for his loving guidance of my mind ever since it first began to think, and of my heart ever since it first began to love.

EDWARD KING 1829–1910 *Sermons and Addresses*

17 *God Makes the World Make Itself*

When we contemplate the physical creation, we see an unimaginable complex, organized on many planes one above another; atomic, molecular, cellular; vegetable, animal, social. And the marvel of it is that at every level the constituent elements run themselves, and, by their mutual interaction, run the world. God not only makes the world, he makes it make itself; or rather, he causes its innumerable constituents to make it. And this in spite of the fact that the constituents are not for the most part intelligent. They cannot enter into the creative purposes they serve. They cannot see beyond the tip of their noses; they have, indeed, no noses not to see beyond, nor any eyes with which to fail in the attempt. All they can do is blind away at being themselves, and fulfil the repetitive pattern of their existence. When you contemplate this amazing structure, do you wonder that it should be full of flaws, breaks, accidents, collisions and disasters? Will you not be more inclined to wonder why chaos does not triumph; how higher forms of organization should ever arise, or, having arisen, maintain and perpetuate themselves?

Though a thousand species have perished with the mammoth and the dodo, and though all species, perhaps, must perish at the last, it is a sort of miracle that the species there are should have established themselves. And how have they established themselves? Science studies the pattern, but theology assigns the cause: that imperceptible persuasion exercised by creative Will on the chaos of natural forces, setting a bias on the positive and achieving the creatures.

AUSTIN FARRER 1904–1968 *Saving Belief*

18 *A Vision of Memory*

The love of Nature is ever returned double to us, not only the delighter in our delight, but by linking our sweetest, but of themselves perishable feelings to distinct and vivid images, which we ourselves, at times, and which a thousand casual recollections, recall to our memory. She is the preserver, the treasurer of our joys. Even in sickness and nervous diseases, she has peopled our imagination with lovely forms which have sometimes overpowered the inward pain and brought with them their old sensations. And even when all men have seemed to desert us and the friend of our heart has passed on, with one glance from his 'cold disliking eye' – yet even then the blue heaven spreads it out and bends over us, and the little tree still shelters us under its plumage as a second cope, a domestic firmament, and the low, creeping gale will sigh in the heath-plant and soothe us by sound of sympathy till the lulled grief lose itself in fixed gaze on the purple heath-blossom, till the present beauty becomes a vision of memory.

SAMUEL TAYLOR COLERIDGE 1772–1834 *Anima Poetae*

19 *The Everlasting Spring*

I went out for a little while on the terrace this morning and walked up and down on the sunny side of the house. After how many illnesses such as this have I taken my first convalescent walk on the sunny terrace and always at this time of year when the honeysuckle leaves were shooting green and the apricot blossoms were dawning and the daffodils in blow. But some day will come the last illness from which there will be no convalescence and after which there will be no going out to enjoy the sweet sights and sounds of the earthly spring, the singing of the birds, the opening of the fruit blossoms, the budding dawn of green leaves, and the blowing of the March daffodils. May I then be prepared to enter into the everlasting Spring and to walk among the birds and flowers of Paradise.

FRANCIS KILVERT 1840–1879 *Kilvert's Diary*

20 *Now Must We Praise*

Now must we praise the Guardian of heaven,
The might of the Lord and his wisdom of mind,
The work of the Father of Glory, maker of all wonders.
He, Holy Creator, first fashioned heaven
As a roof for the sons of men.
Then the eternal Guardian of mankind
Adorned the earth below, a land for men,
Almighty King and everlasting Lord.

CAEDMON *d. c.* 680

Hymn: For the Beauty of the Earth

For the beauty of the earth,
  For the beauty of the skies,
For the love which from our birth
  Over and around us lies,
Lord of all, to thee we raise
This our grateful hymn of praise.

For the beauty of each hour
  Of the day and of the night,
Hill and vale, and tree and flower,
  Sun and moon and stars of light,
Lord of all, to thee we raise
This our grateful hymn of praise.

For the joy of human love,
  Brother, sister, parent, child,
Friends on earth, and friends above,
  Pleasures pure and undefiled,
Lord of all, to thee we raise
This our grateful hymn of praise.

For each perfect gift of thine,
  To our race so freely given,
Graces human and divine,
  Flowers of earth and buds of heaven,
Lord of all, to thee we raise
This our grateful hymn of praise.

For thy Church which evermore
  Lifteth holy hands above,
Offering up on every shore
  Her pure sacrifice of love,
Lord of all, to thee we raise
This our grateful hymn of praise.

F. S. PIERPOINT 1835–1917

Acknowledgements

We gratefully acknowledge permission to reprint copyright material in this anthology. We apologize to those copyright holders whom it has proved impossible to locate.

George Appleton: from *Journey for a Soul*, Fount Paperbacks, Collins Publishers, 1977. Reprinted by permission of the publisher.

Adrian Bell: from *The Cherry Tree*, The Bodley Head, 1948. Reprinted by permission of the publisher.

Catherine Bramwell-Booth: from *Letters* introduced by Mary Batchelor, Lion publishing PLC. 1986. Reprinted by permission of the publisher.

Gerald Bullett: from *Poems*, Cambridge University Press, 1949. Reprinted by permission of Rosemary Seymour.

Robert Byron: from *Little Innocents*, The Bodley Head, 1932.

Geoffrey Chaucer: from *The Canterbury Tales* translated by Nevill Coghill, Penguin Books, 1977. Reprinted by permission of the publisher.

Agatha Christie: from *Poems*, Collins Publishers, 1973. Reprinted by permission of Aitken & Stone Ltd.

Kenneth Clark: from *Animals and Men*, Thames & Hudson Ltd, 1977. Reprinted by permission of the publisher.

J. M. C. Crum: from *The Oxford Book of Carols*, Oxford University Press, 1964. Reprinted by permission of the publisher.

Gerald Durrell: from *My Family and Other Animals*, Penguin Books, 1959. Reprinted by permission of Harper Collins Publishers Ltd.

Albert Einstein: from *Ideas and Opinions*, Souvenir Press, 1973. Reprinted by permission of Souvenir Press Ltd and Crown Publishers Inc.

Austin Farrer: from *Saving Belief*, Hodder & Stoughton Ltd, 1967. Reprinted by permission of the publisher.

Paul Gallico: from *The Snow Goose*, Michael Joseph Ltd, 1941. Reprinted by permission of Aitken & Stone Ltd.

Robert Gibbings: from *Sermons by Artists*, Golden Cockerel Press, 1934. Reprinted by permission of the publishers.

Ernest Hemingway: from *The Old Man and the Sea*, Jonathan Cape, 1952. Reprinted by permission of George V. Bobrinskoy Jr. and the Hemingway Foreign Trust.

Susan Hill: from *The Magic Apple Tree*, Hamish Hamilton Ltd, 1982. Reprinted by permission of the publisher.

Helen Hoover: from *The Long-Shadowed Forest*, Souvenir Press, 1963.

Fred Hoyle: *The Nature of the Universe*, Basil Blackwell & Mott Ltd, 1960.

Anthony Huxley: from *Plant and Planet*, Penguin Books, 1987. Reprinted by permission of the publisher.

Julian Huxley: from *Religion Without Revelation*, C. A. Watts Ltd, 1941.

W. R. Inge: from *Outspoken Essays*, Longman, Green & Co. Ltd, 1922. Reprinted by permission of the Longman Group UK Ltd.

Francis Kilvert: from *Kilvert's Diary* edited by William Plomer, Jonathan Cape, 1944. Reprinted by permission of the editor and Mrs Sheila Hooper.

Laurie Lee: from *Cider with Rosie*, Chatto & Windus, 1959. Reprinted by permission of the publisher.

C. S. Lewis: from *Transposition and Other Essays*, Fontana Paperbacks, Collins Publishers, 1949. Reprinted by permission of the publisher.

Eiluned Lewis: from *Dew on the Grass*, The Boydell Press, 1984. Reprinted by permission of Mrs Katrina Burnett.

Hugh Lofting: from *The Voyages of Doctor Doolittle*, Puffin Books, 1967.

H. J. Massingham: from *Wold Without End*, R. Cobden-Sanderson, 1932.

Gervase Mathew: from *Byzantine Aesthetics*, John Murray Ltd, 1963. Reprinted by permission of the publisher.

Thomas Merton: from *The New Man*, Burns & Oates Ltd, 1962. Reprinted by permission of the publisher.

Christopher Milne: from *The Enchanted Places*, Methuen Books, 1974. Reprinted by permission of the publisher and Curtis Brown, London.

Edwin Muir: from *An Autobiography*, The Hogarth Press Ltd, 1954. Reprinted by permission of the publisher and Gavin Muir.

Edwin Mullins: from *A Love Affair with Nature*, Phaidon Press Ltd, 1985. Reprinted by permission of the publisher.

Kathleen Raine: from *Collected Poems*, Hamish Hamilton Ltd, 1952. Reprinted by permission of the publisher.

Michael Ramsey: from *Through the Year with Michael Ramsey* edited by

Margaret Duggen, Hodder & Stoughton Ltd, 1975. Reprinted by permission of Edward England Books.

George Santayana: from *Little Essays*, Constable & Co. Ltd, 1920. Reprinted by permission of the publisher.

Dorothy L. Sayers: from *The Zeal of thy House*, Victor Gollancz Ltd, 1952. Reprinted by permission of David Higham Associates Ltd.

Stevie Smith: from *The Collected Poems of Stevie Smith*, edited by James MacGibbon, Penguin Modern Classics, 1985. Reprinted by permission of the editor.

F. S. Smythe: from *Climbs and Ski Runs*, William Blackwood & Sons Ltd, 1929.

John Steinbeck: from *The Red Pony*, William Heinemann Ltd, 1937. Reprinted by permission of the publisher.

Arthur Symons: from *Cities and Sea-Coasts and Islands*, Collins Publishers, 1918. Reprinted by permission of Harper Collins Ltd.

William Temple: from *Nature, Man and God*, Macmillan & Co. Ltd, 1934. Reprinted by permission of the publisher.

R. S. Thomas: from *Poetry for Supper*, Rupert Hart-Davis, 1958. Reprinted by permission of Gwydion Thomas.

J. R. R. Tolkien: from *The Lord of the Rings*, George Allen & Unwin, 1954. Reprinted by permission of Unwin Hyman Ltd.

Evelyn Underhill: from *Worship*, Nisbet & Co. Ltd, 1943.

Robert Way: from *The Garden of the Beloved*, Sheldon Press, 1975. Reprinted by permission of SPCK.

Alfred North Whitehead: from *Dialogues of Alfred North Whitehead* as recorded by Lucien Price, Max Reinhardt, 1954. Reprinted by permission of the publisher.

Virginia Woolf: from *To the Lighthouse*, Penguin Books, 1964. Reprinted by permission of Chatto & Windus and The Hogarth Press.

The quotations from the Bible are taken from the Authorized Version.

In addition we wish to thank Maureen Beresford, Diana Osborn, Valerie Peters and Hazel Rowbottom for their help in compiling this anthology.

The illustrations at the beginning of each chapter are taken from woodcuts by Thomas Bewick and his school.

Index